150

TYPE —ONE

36

discipline and
progress
in typography

CONTENT   **TYPE ONE**

In the age of mass communication, type as a medium is subject to
complex, multidimensional demands and requirements. These are often
contradictory in their form and intention, which leads to new design
criteria and increasingly complex disciplines. The actual difficulty of
modern typeface design now lies in separating out and selecting
necessary accents from the infinite pool of considered, rejected,
historical and modern fonts, i.e. in more or less consciously integrating
the fundamentals of type and typography as they have evolved and
developed over the millennia. Type One goes back to this pool and
selects examples to present and take stock of current varieties and
trends in typography and typeface design.

CONTENT

TITLE   INTRODUCTION
AUTHOR   SILJA BILZ
CHARACTERS   12.774

Type is communication. Writing is a sign language, an independent thought- and knowledge-communicating medium and method. Writing provides a universal copy of mankind's memory. It captures both the written and the unwritten: "intellegere", intelligent reading between the lines. The philosopher Karl Popper[1] addresses the specifically human function of language and thus "especially of its daughter, human writing". He identifies three functional steps: the lowest is called *expressive function*; the second establishes *communication* and includes the first (applying equally to animals and human beings). The third function[2], *descriptive function* is "reserved for specifically human language, which works in sentences that describe facts". Writing, as the daughter of human language, is thus language made visual. Type is also image. Typography means both organising typeface design visually and designing characters and realising them technically. Typographic design aims to unify the written word and language, content and form. Script – originally a direct expression of living thought, feeling and communication – is inextricably linked in its formal language with mankind's social development. Type is a repertoire of defined signs whose meaning is based on agreements forged over the centuries. So if the reading process is to function, it is essential to recognise and identify these signs. Thus the anatomy of a type, the inner structure of a letter, is prescribed within a particular culture. This is why in our roman alphabet the shapes of individual letters can be changed only within strict limits, to enable optimal decoding. Meanings are allotted to sequences of letters (semantics). Merely recognising words is more or less automatic. Often the meaning of a visual image, for example, can be deciphered only partially and slowly, while the meaning of a written word is perceived precisely and quickly. As in the case of the spoken word, a purely rational grasp is impossible here. Visual perception of reading matter is complex; it also has sensual-emotional and aesthetic components. Visual signals always trigger associations and sensations relating to subjective engrams (memory content) that can be deliberately influenced by the external structuring of the letters and the typographic design. Non-verbal concepts that can be conveyed by speech modulation (tone, expression) can also be adequately expressed visually using typographical devices (weight, style etc.). The degree of impact made – influenced by the dimensions, organisation and accentuation of a typeface – is indeed determined by the type designer's intentions, but crucially by the targets and function (body text, headline, screen etc.) that the client or author have in mind. So the perception process is complex. Popper, emphasising the relationship between specifically human speech and writing, speaks of a profound "innate need for suggestion, specifically linked with language", in order to "coincide" with the wishes and evaluations of "communicating with fellow members of the species". Thus, logically, the "daughter" of human language seems inseparably linked with human evolution and recent history. Every historically evolved typeface reflects architecture, technical and cultural achievements, (see also writing implements, materials) that are closely linked with the human spirit of a particular age, and convey a sensual and aesthetic insight into that age. Type cannot actually be reinvented, only its outer form and basic framework can be modified.

Cuneiform script (about 3000 BC) marks the first time we can speak of writing. But the first numerical representations and signs can be dated to about 30,000 BC. Laws, treaties and commercial communications are fixed in writing in the surviving examples of the Sumerian cuneiform (word and syllabic). The way there and onwards passed through several stages over the millennia: pictures, picture-signs (pictograms), concept signs (ideograms) and hieroglyphics. The world's first verifiable alphabet, from which our roman alphabet also derives, goes back to the Phoenicians in about 1200 BC (suggested by the Egyptian hieroglyphic system). The Greeks took over the 22 consonants of the Phoenician phonetic script and added vowels. In this way they developed an alphabet that has helped to shape many Western script systems to a considerable extent. The basis of the capital, or upper-case, letters that are still used in our roman alphabet is the *Capitalis Monumentalis* perfected by the Romans, or the *Capitalis Quadrata*, which was taken over as a book script. But the small, or lower-case, letters in our roman alphabet are derived from the so-called *Carolingian Minuscule* (about 800 BC), which developed under Charlemagne into a universally accepted script that was easy to write and read. *Carolingian Minuscule* led among other things to *Gothic Minuscule* (13th century AD), a closely, rapidly written script made up of letters set close together with black lines and a grid-like structure, also a precursor of German black-letter, Fractura or Gothic script (16th century). In 1440, the coin-maker and goldsmith Johannes Gensfleisch zur Laden, commonly known as Gutenberg, invented movable metal type. We have his invention to thank among other things for the fact that we are able to put individual letters together to make printable pages, and to reproduce them. Thus Gutenberg forged a path from written matter to set type, which could be used to copy thinking and knowledge mechanically. Gutenberg remained committed to the black-letter principle with his *Textura* Bible typeface, but at the same time, in Venice, so-called "Antiqua" (roman) was developed as a new printed script form, which still forms the basis of our roman alphabet today. The Renaissance humanists' concern (from the 15th century) to return to the Greek and Roman models of antiquity also affected the forms of roman face, which first combined capital and small letters. Going back to ancient forms, roman face evolved from *Capitalis Quadrata,* and the capitals and small letters of Carolingian (Humanist) Minuscule. So the formal canon of our modern roman alphabet goes back to two fundamentally different sources. The Renaissance also saw Arabic numerals included in what is now our alphabet. One of the most impressive of the old-style typefaces from the French Renaissance is *Garamond*, by the type-cutter Claude Garamond. The characteristics of this typeface are the low contrast between hair lines and stems, the soft overall line (derived from pen-strokes) and the left-inclined axis of the round forms. Baroque typefaces (mid-17th century) show greater contrasts between hair and stem lines, the axes of the round letters are less oblique and the serifs finer (*Janson Text*). Thus they form the transition from Renaissance to neoclassical roman, Modern Typefaces. These latter faces show the influence of copperplate engraving, which enables strong and clear formal contrasts between hair and stem lines. New forms are constructed; the type axis stands vertically, the sense of handwriting has disappeared. These typefaces (17th and 18th century) were largely developed by the Didot family of printers and the Italian, Giambattista Bodoni, and in the early-19th-century by the German, Erich Wahlbaum. General standardisation at this time also led to new standards in typography (e.g. the typographical point system). Industrialisation in the early-19th century brought slab-serif typefaces in Britain, with little or no difference between hair and stem lines, and emphasised or monumental-looking serifs. The first sans-serif typefaces also developed in Britain around this time, something that had not existed until then. The technical look, and the apparently uniform line thicknesses, without serif brackets (see also the simplified form of "g"), were seen as "grotesque" by their contemporaries, hence the name. These new typefaces (e.g. Akzidenz Grotesk) were used at first exclusively for setting titles and headlines for posters and advertisements (display typography). Lithography in particular – as a new reproduction technique – led to the literal liberation of type-forms. It was now technically possible to reproduce hand-drawn fonts and free letter-forms in print.

The 20th century changed the whole medium of type. At first, historical ideas were particularly important; rivalries broke out between different styles and tendencies, presentation and reproduction techniques. Radically aesthetic artistic movements and counter-movements (Dadaism, Constructivism, etc.) on the one hand, and typographic designs that were merely craft-oriented on the other, fought to hold their own alongside classical book typography. Type was increasingly moving out of the realm of printed matter. For example, the "Elementare Typografie" of the 1920s experimented with formal clarity of expression and geometrically constructed sans-serif forms with no flourishes (Futura, Gill etc.). In the mid-20th century, Grotesque underwent a revival. It became the model for new, "modulated" alphabets that deviated from the formal principle as originally constructed. Adrian Frutiger published his *Univers* and Max Miedinger cut his *Helvetica*, modelled on *Akzidenz Grotesk*. A new era in typography began in the 1970s. Within a decade, as a result of the introduction of the optical-mechanical typesetting system (photo-setting), hot-metal setting, now 500 years old, had practically disappeared. In the late-20th century the mass media produced a wide range of universal typefaces and design approaches; *Frutiger*, hybrid types (*Stone, Rotis* etc.). Technical innovations (PC, Apple Computer, DTP, World Wide Web) revolutionised type as a medium, causing conventions to be reconsidered and broken down; entirely new paths were explored. Type abandoned its traditional support materials and conquered cyberspace. Characters were no longer analogue, but above all, digital. Type culture underwent a hitherto unheard-of structural change that was to influence our reading and viewing habits more or less permanently. Type, almost a dematerialised medium that can be reproduced at will, seemed to make everything possible – everything was tried. Freedom in design was rediscovered – typography and type were democratised. Hard- and software were universally available, so practically anyone could work with his or her own typeface, generate it or modify a familiar one. Typefaces became popular. Recourse to history brought success for new typographical adapta-

tions and impulses; epoch-making type-styles were collected and re-assessed, archaic motifs illustrated or anticipated appropriately in terms of typography. Type, font technology and the font market ultimately showed inflationary traits, but these also provoked new challenges, approaches and technologies (PostScript-Type 1 etc.). Type-forms adapted for screens and pixels were produced for reading on monitors. For economic and contemporary aesthetic reasons, typefaces for body texts became increasingly narrow, their mid-lengths higher and their forms more open.

In the age of mass communication, the demands and needs that type had to meet as a medium became ever more complex, multi-dimensional, and often had contradictory implications and intentions. This led to new design criteria and increasingly complex disciplines. The actual difficulty of modern typographic design now lies in differentiating and in choosing necessary accents from the infinite pool of considered, rejected, historical and modern type-forms, i.e. in the more or less deliberate integration of the basic principles of type and typography that have matured and developed over the centuries. *Type One* goes back to this pool, and selects examples to present and take stock of current varieties and tendencies in typography and typeface design.

TITLE   GOLDEN RULES / HOW DO I DEVELOP A GOOD TEXT TYPEFACE?
AUTHOR   SILIJA BILZ
CHARACTERS   9.439

Reading means consciously perceiving and absorbing subject matter, and also unconsciously perceiving the printed letter-form that is conveying the subject matter. If this reading process is to work as well as possible, basic technical skills are needed when developing a text face, along with knowledge of the interplay between visual perception phenomena.

1.
Aims: First determine the purpose for which the type is to be used, and the technical requirements.

2.
Regularity and differentiation: A typeface is an homogeneous unity made up of different characters; formally it must present a uniform image (rhythmical details, equal terminals, visually equal main stroke weights, very similar bowls etc.). But the basic forms should not be too similar, to make it easier to distinguish them from each other; a balance has to be struck.

3.
Basic framework for the letters: The letters **H** and **n** convey the essential qualities of a font. They determine height and the basic proportions (line weight, width, counters, stroke starts, terminals, shoulders, bowls etc.).

4.
Letter weight: The weight of the lower-case letters is less than that of the upper-case letters.

5.
Letter width: The **m** must not be a double **n**; the counter of the **o** must correspond with the optical width of the **n**; the **u** should always be slightly narrower than the **n**.

6.
Round forms: Letters with horizontal arches (e.g. **o**) must come above or below the imaginary typeface lines (otherwise they look too small as a whole).

7.
Ascenders and descenders: The descenders in a typeface should never be shorter than the ascenders. The ascenders of the lower-case letters (e.g. **l**, **f**) should always be slightly above the capitals.

8.
Height of the bars: The bar of an **H** is in the visual, rather than the mathematical, centre. This applies to all horizontally divided letters (**A**, **B**, **K**, **S**, **x** etc.).

9.
Diagonal strokes and weights: Upward diagonal strokes (e.g. **A**, **N**) are thinner than downward strokes in order to make the same optical effect. Free-ending diagonal bars (e.g. **z**) taper towards the meeting-point. The lines in the cross of the **X** are not drawn through as straight lines, but are offset from each other and run slightly conically to the meeting-point. Horizontal bars are always drawn narrower than the stems, so that they look the same optically.

10.
The character set: A font has more characters than the 26 letters of the alphabet; numerals, punctuation and other figure-groups have to be matched to the overall picture.

11.
Spacing a text font: Individual letters are not yet a set. Obtrusive holes, or unduly narrow spacing between letters and words make it difficult to recognise words and sentences as a whole, and thus make the font less easy to read fluently. Spacing means creating optically equal distances between letters (matching point size, character width, counters and main line weight). Basic spacing is applied to the letters **H**, **n**, **o** and **0**.

12.
Kerning a text font: The more carefully a font has been spaced and the concept of the character forms devised, the less effort will be needed in the kerning process. But kerning is essential to create optically equal-looking white spaces for certain pairs of letters. The rule of kerning is that only the most important pairs of letters (e.g. **AT**, **AV**, **Av**, **AC**, **DY**, **FA**) should be kerned.

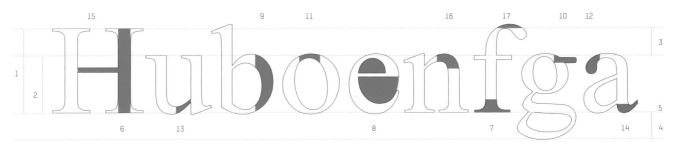

Weight of letter: weight type; line weight; rule weight; relative darkness of the characters in the various typefaces (e.g. regular, bold, heavy).

Type angle: slope of letter; Italic, Regular, Oblique.

Black width: horizontal distance from leftmost to rightmost of a letterform, not including the white space (e.g. condensed, regular, expanded).

Width: of a character; horizontal distance including white space on either side (left and right sidebearing); advance width

Spacing: character spacing, character fit; balancing the distances of the letters from each other, arising from the left and right sidebearing of a letter; determining running width.

Kerning: pair kerning; to add or remove white space between two pairs of letters, improve visual appearance, legibility in specific pairs of letters (e.g. AT, VA).

Counter: the space inside a letter.

Lower-case letter: the small letters in a typeface.

Capitals: upper-case letters, the large letters in a typeface.

Serifs: "little feet" endings, decorative strokes, forms added to the end of a letter's main strokes.

Italics: italic type; script-like version, closer to handwriting.

Oblique: similar to italics, slanting version of a upright (roman) face without the script quality; simple electronic manipulations of the roman forms.

Character set: all the characters in a font (e.g. letters, accent, punctuation, numerals).

Punctuation marks: stops and other signs inserted in text.

x-height: height of the lower-case letters.

1 cap height
2 x-height
3 ascender
4 descender
5 baseline, typelines
6 stem
7 serif
8 counter
9 bowl

10 ear
11 stress, arch
12 ball
13 link
14 terminal
15 bar
16 shoulder
17 kern, overhang, overshoot

CONVERSATION   WENDELIN HESS, BEAT MÜLLER, WOLFGANG WEINGART
AUTHOR   MAX BRUINSMA
CHARACTERS   14.286

Never before have so many new typefaces been designed and published as in the last decade or two. How do designers cope with such abundance? We asked three Swiss designers who have made a name as typographers – not by making letters, but by using them. Wolfgang Weingart is as famous for cutting up letters and testing the boundaries of readability, as he is an advocate of thorough knowledge the fundamentals of typography. In a sense he can be seen as someone who, by merely adjusting or distorting type, paved the way for a generation who took tinkering with letters to the next stage; sampling them from different sources. Beat Müller and Wendelin Hess work together as Müller+Hess, combining thorough Basel-typography training with enjoying handling typefaces experimentally. Again, they don't design their own fonts, but adjust them when they feel the need for it. The three agree about one other thing; they use a very limited number of typefaces.

Wolfgang Weingart: I can manage with a very small number of typefaces. And a lot of these so-called new typefaces aren't new anyway. Their great inventors are no longer known. If you look at a 1930s Max Bill alphabet it could be one of today's.
Wendelin Hess: Possibly we don't know where they came from any more, but these old, experimental typefaces are being digitalised today, and so they are visible again, and can be used. And then there are anonymous typefaces from old posters and advertisements that are now used as a basis for new fonts. One example: the *Brauer* typeface (Elektrosmog 1999) is based on a Zurich brewery's old Corporate Identity, and it's an attractive font. I could imagine finding some appealing creative uses on this basis. But what I find more important than this "old" or "new" question is how these typefaces are used; you can divide the whole of typeface history into typefaces that dominate application and typefaces that subordinate themselves to application.
Max Bruinsma: Could you use *Brauer* without pointing out the typeface's cultural background? Surely it has an atmosphere about it that does not necessarily have to go back to the brewery, but nevertheless recognisably evokes a particular era and also a certain origin.
Wendelin Hess: This typeface is so simple and reticent that it can still be used today, detached from its original context. It seems more timeless than other typefaces. If you use another typeface that is formally more assertive, it will dominate every job you use it for. In other words, you don't get anything out of deciding to use this typeface. Everything looks the same in *Moonbase Alpha*, to use a common, crude example. But if I use a reduced typeface, whether it's *Helvetica* or this brewery typeface, this decision forces me to devise a structure that becomes a key quality, because the typeface itself fades into the background. Look at our "Art Basel" catalogue, for example; you can swap the typefaces around there and the book wouldn't be any worse.

Max Bruinsma: The whole thing in *Univers*, that would definitely be another book altogether!
Beat Müller: It would certainly make a slightly different impression. But we're talking about a succinct concept here, not whether it's in *Franklin Gothic* or a similar grotesque typeface.
Max Bruinsma: So there are typefaces that carry their own design programme within them. The built-in programme will dominate everything else.
Wolfgang Weingart: Exactly! The main problem for me with a lot of these new typefaces is that they really are personal statements. They are made by designers, for their own works.
Wendelin Hess: And when you use these typefaces the creative achievement is more to do with the typeface designer than the designer of the publication. We were always more interested in modifying existing typefaces than designing completely new fonts. We were more concerned to adapt typefaces to our needs and to optimize them within a specific context.
Wolfgang Weingart: There are some amusing typefaces, but my problems are quite different. I want to express myself typographically with the least possible effort and thus achieve maximum quality. I can make very good typography with a hundred-year-old typewriter typeface. I don't need any substitute for that. You have to know the fundamentals. I'm a classicist in that respect, I believe in it; if you had not worked your way through the fundamentals as designers you would not be what you are today.
Max Bruinsma: What you're essentially saying is that we should train good experts who'll be able to keep up with developments beyond tomorrow. But whether you like it or not, it's possible to say quite neutrally that our entire culture is focused on "today". Design statements are statements for "now", about how the world looks "today", and not about our branch of the industry, not about continuity.
Wolfgang Weingart: But we have to keep on thinking ahead. Thinking back *and* thinking ahead. Crossing out, for example, is not my invention, I regenerated it. When you were in Basel everything was forbidden. You were the *enfants terribles* at college, rightly, just as I was thrown out in 1964 for organising lectures against this rigid interpretation of typography and graphics. You grew up as if you were in a monastery, didn't you? And then you rebelled, and I think that's great!
Beat Müller: It is interesting to see how strongly this constraint produced a counter-reaction. A good example, that's nothing to do with typography would be our attempted resistance to the college's rigid colour theories. We used papers with 30 different pre-printed colours for the posters for the 30th Basel Art. We didn't do the colour composition in the street, that was up to the billposter, using his best judgement. It produced some interesting combinations that we

couldn't have put together ourselves. We were striking a blow against school-like, laborious converging and matching of colours.

Wolfgang Weingart: But the Basel philosophy still shines through these Basel Art posters, a Hofmann-esque colour minimalism. Most people from the Hofmann school just carried on like him, only a few managed to transform things into a new kind of symbolism. I can see Hofmann's minimalism in your posters, that's a subconscious further processing of the fundamentals you learned at the time.

Beat Müller: It is also an attempt to get away from these traditional design processes. We want to recognise or invent a principle that develops of its own accord; so that we don't have to keep pushing things around for hours on end – the typeface a point smaller or larger here, everything a bit to the left or the right there. Once we have found our parameters, and they are well designed, we can leave them to combinatorial chance, and it works as a rule, as in the printed matter for the cascade condenser, for example [ill. p. 12].

Wendelin Hess: A set of instruments always generates random features and mistakes that can be used. You turn knobs and a hundred pages of dreadful material come out; but somewhere or other there is a key. Random features and mistakes are the raw material in our design process.

Max Bruinsma: I think that's a typical computer generation approach. You have an instrument here that can achieve this kind of logical consistency. And you can also see that, for this generation, typeface form has become part of the whole *message*.

Wendelin Hess: This technology also made it possible to build pictorial elements into fonts. In *Meccano* (Ludvic Balland, 2003), for example, every letter has its own decoration, which creates its expressive quality, but that quality works differently in the typeface's formal language from the way it works in the underlying alphabet. Something similar happened in our pictorial alphabet for "Eye Magazine" (Eye #32, 1999). There we replaced every letter with a picture series – cars, naked women, Popes etc. This produced a text that could only be read through belonging to a picture-family. This probably hasn't got much to do with typography and is in fact illegible, but it is an interesting starting-point for new, more concrete applications.

Max Bruinsma: It has something directly to do with typography; if only for the reason that picture become signs here. What I find interesting is merging image and text, pictures and letters. Images become letters or words by means of iconic condensation, and letters or words become images through their formal characteristics. That's something that does not often crop up in your work; you use mainly typefaces that are relatively neutral, to make your statement.

Wendelin Hess: Our reduction is also about the fact that we work in fields were maximum legibility is a priority. You say, Wolfgang, "we've got enough typefaces, leave it alone". But I am very happy with *Lexicon*, a relatively new typeface by Bram de Does and Peter Mathias

Noodzij (The Entschede Font Factory, 1994), which has qualities that we have not found in this combination with any other typeface.

Beat Müller: There are a lot of very good reading typefaces, but they usually give you a sense of the time they come from. That's why I find it interesting that we don't just have "Zeitgeist" typefaces, but typefaces that are really new and legible as well.

Wendelin Hess: And there's another thing, if you have a neutral typeface that's formally attractive and complete, you can modify this typeface as a designer. For example, we used *Bell* as the title typeface for the Tagesanzeiger's "Das Magazin", but took the characteristic serifs off the capital "I". These serifs were too strong a visual identification for us – you could see straight away, that's *Bell*. But after we'd taken these tiny serifs off, scarcely anyone recognised the typeface. And for example, we also shortened the descenders and ascenders in *Trade Gothic*, because it improved legibility in a particular application for a client. I think it's effective to find your way to new independent qualities through little emergency operations like these.

Wolfgang Weingart: *Berthold* is still a good typeface, but even *Berthold* has had some less than attractive features, and then I just cut them off because I didn't like them. The principle is the same. I am more interested in the problems posed by reading than in this or that typeface: how can we read more quickly, how can we reduce the alphabet to 16 rather than 22 or 26 letters'. These are questions I'm thinking about at the moment. How can we take in a publication really quickly, rather than ploughing laboriously through it? Something brilliant came out of a piece of research in Cambridge. It showed that only the first and last letters of a word have to be right for it to be possible to read it, the other letters can be distributed at random. That is brilliant!

Max Bruinsma: I think that a lot of the experiment's of younger generation of "fontographers" work subconsciously through what these Cambridge experiments have shown; we don't read letters, we read words. You recognise word-pictures, as on the cover of your book, for example.

Wolfgang Weingart: The book was actually supposed to be trilingual, and you can read the title word "typography" in all languages, it's just written differently at the end, sometimes with "y", sometimes with "ie" or just "i", or with "ph" or "f". That's why I could cut off more at the end. Things like that always derive from quite simple circumstances. I reduce; black, white or tyepwriter, or I cut something off or up; I still find that absolutely fascinating.

Max Bruinsma: Is it possible to say that what was traditionally done with combinations of different fonts or with variations on the same font, and that's now built-in as part of the font's formal expression, that you do that more or less outside the font. You use 26 letters, and what you do with these letters is you accentuate them – not a quality of the font, but something added by you.

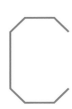

CONVERSATION   WENDELIN HESS, BEAT MÜLLER, WOLFGANG WEINGART
AUTHOR   MAX BRUINSMA
CHARACTERS   14.286

Wolfgang Weingart: Exactly; and that's why I'd like to use an alphabet that's archaic, that's uncomplicated, and – very importantly – that's very neutral in its expression. In this way I can express my own new ideas more strongly because I am using uncomplicated elements.

Wendelin Hess: Elements that don't distract from the matter in hand. An interesting typographical idea works well with a neutral typeface, but I couldn't really care less whether it's typeface A, typeface B or typeface C. Or a typeface that has to be optimised for a particular application. Staging a change can go so far that we say every letter has five points underneath, whether it's a wide "w" or a narrow "i". This produces interesting patterns that structure the application. Ultimately as typeface users we are interested in creating independence, identity. And you can't do that by just using *Times*.

Wolfgang Weingart: What we're talking about is very interesting, but it's very unimportant as well. What we do is the odd millimetre here and there, and that has pretty well nothing to do with what's going on around us. When you go out in the street people are on about quite different things, Iraq or God knows what. We just have to be careful not to exaggerate the importance of what we do. These are mainly questions of attitude. The most important thing is to commit to a particular attitude and enjoy your work.

DESIGN   MÜLLER+HESS
CLIENT   NEUE MUSIK RÜMLIGEN, MEDIA LUZ, MUSIC FESTIVAL (CH)
PROJECT   POSTER AND MAGAZIN, 1997

DESIGN   MÜLLER+HESS
CLIENT   ART BASEL, INTERNATIONAL ART SHOW
PROJECT   NEW CORPORATE IDENTITY, NEW CATALOG DESIGN 99/00

—
DESIGN   MÜLLER+HESS
CLIENT   GALLERY KASKADENKONDENSATOR (BASEL, CH)
PROJECT   INVITATIONCARDS AND POSTER 97/98

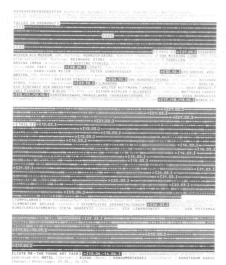

—
DESIGN   MÜLLER+HESS
CLIENT   "EYE", THE INTERNATIONAL REVIEW OF GRAPHIC DESIGN,
            NR.32, VOL. 8, SUMMER 99 (LONDON UK)
PROJECT   "THE IMPOSSIBILITY OF NEUTRALITY", PICTURE-FONT

—
DESIGN   MÜLLER+HESS
CLIENT   MUSEUM FÜR GESTALTUNG, ZÜRICH (CH)
PROJECT   INVITATIONCARDS AND POSTER 99/00 FOR EXHIBITION
            "RICHARD PAUL LOHSE"

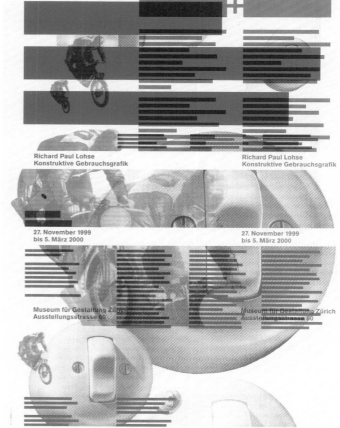

—
DESIGN
CREDIT

WOLFGANG WEINGART
EXERCISE INITIATED BY KIM MEYER ANDERSEN. REFINED
AND DEVELOPED IN THE SEVENTIES BY MARTIN SOMMER.

—
DESIGN
CREDIT

WOLFGANG WEINGART
COVER DESIGN AND INSIDE SPREADS FOR PROJEKTE.
TYPOGRAPHIC RESEARCH AT THE BASEL SCHOOL OF DESIGN
PUBLISHED BY ARTHUR NIGGLI.

—
DESIGN
CREDIT

WOLFGANG WEINGART
COVER DESIGN FROM THE BOOK TYPOGRAPHY,
MY WAY TO TYPOGRAPHY PUBLISHED BY LARS MÜLLER.

Projekte.

Weingart:
Ergebnisse aus dem Typographie-Unterricht an
der Kunstgewerbeschule Basel, Schweiz.

| Projekt I | James Faris.
Werkzeug, Arbeitsmethode: Eine ‹typogra-
phische› Bildkonfrontation in 26 Collagen. | Vorwort
von Armin Hofmann |
| Projekt II | Gregory Vines.
Das Tor in Bellinzona: Ideen, Skizzen, Ent-
würfe. Die 6 Umschläge für die
‹Typographischen Monatsblätter› 1978. | |

Projects.

Weingart:
Typographic Research at the School of Design
Basle, Switzerland.

| Project I | James Faris.
Tool, Process, Sensibility: Images of Typo-
graphy in 26 Collages. | Introduction
by Armin Hofmann |
| Project II | Gregory Vines,
The Gate in Bellinzona: Ideas, Sketches and
Designs. The 6 Covers for the
‹Typographische Monatsblaetter›, 1978. | |

Verlag Arthur Niggli AG

Weingart:

TYPO
GRAPHY

Lars Müller Publishers

1

A display face is characteristically unique, arresting, pictorial, uniform, provocative and/or expressive. Its specific task is to demonstrate presence. The typographical concept "display face" covers typefaces that are usually large, primarily intended for headlines, titles and headings, or for emphasis. A wide variety is available, ranging from subtly refined to radically wild. Display and headline faces can form independent text units or support the body text. The key feature is the directly perceived outward impression made by the type or the words. Everything seems reasonable – and that is precisely their charm. Typography becomes an expressive medium that is being deliberately emphasised. Display faces are ideal for conveying moods visually. If expressiveness or originality are central, this usually happens at the expense of legibility, but without making the message any less lucid. Infringements of the laws of harmony also take their toll. Often a single set of lettering or even individual letters are developed for a headline, and the rest of the alphabet is ignored. Neutrally reticent typefaces tend to be favoured for titles, but bolder faces from existing text typefaces can be used. If type is related directly to an advertised product, it takes on a deliberate function that serves a particular purpose; its appearance conveys product-related associations, qualities, emotions and evaluations as a uniform visual message that – once it has been determined – is intended to be recognised again. No generally valid trends seem to be emerging overall; the days of open revolution seem to be gone; various varieties coexist. Every company, every subculture, every medium creates its own typographical and aesthetic standards and codes. Processes of seeing and perceiving are influenced by this, but are not fundamentally changed.

DISPLAY

DESIGN   NEUBAU / STEFAN GANDL
TYPE   NBSTICK
TYPEDESIGN   NEUBAU / STEFAN GANDL (INSPIRED BY THE WORK OF MARKUS DRESSEN)
CREDIT   JPEOPLE MAGAZINE IS ARTDIRECTED BY A ROOM FOR ROMEO STORM

DESIGN   NEUBAU / STEFAN GANDL
TYPE   NBSTICK
TYPEDESIGN   NEUBAU / STEFAN GANDL (INSPIRED BY THE WORK OF MARKUS DRESSEN)
CREDIT   JPEOPLE MAGAZINE IS ARTDIRECTED BY A ROOM FOR ROMEO STORM

DESIGN   NEUBAU / STEFAN GANDL
TYPE   NBSTICK
TYPEDESIGN   NEUBAU / STEFAN GANDL (INSPIRED BY THE WORK OF MARKUS DRESSEN)
CREDIT   JPEOPLE MAGAZINE IS ARTDIRECTED BY A ROOM FOR ROMEO STORM

jpeople

brand file 1 (spring & summer 2004) EUR 8,50
43 brands, 45 gadgets, 505 items

featuring: **A room for Romeo TM Storm. Carsten Fock, Stefan Gandl (Neubau Berlin), Daniel Haaksman,**
Elena Zenero-Hock, Sabine Mühlbauer, Thomas Tritsch (Morgen Furniture), Anna Rose, Shantel,
Nada Nadia Vagioka, Mengstu Zeleke.

DESIGN   NEUBAU / STEFAN GANDL
TYPE   NBSTICK
TYPEDESIGN   NEUBAU / STEFAN GANDL (INSPIRED BY THE WORK OF MARKUS DRESSEN)
CREDIT   JPEOPLE MAGAZINE IS ARTDIRECTED BY A ROOM FOR ROMEO STORM

17

TYPE NB 55RMS
TYPEDESIGN NEUBAU / STEFAN GANDL
DISTRIBURTOR WWW.NEUBAULADEN.COM

2002

[16

ABCDEFGHIJKLMNOPQRSTUVWXYZ
0123456789-(.,:?+!) «€» [/]&ß<>

[8 / 9.5

LOREM IPSUM DOLOR SIT AMET, CONSECTETUER
ADIPISCING ELIT, SED DIAM NONUMMY NIBH
EUISMOD TINCIDUNT UT LAOREET DOLORE MAGNA
ALIQUAM ERAT VOLUTPAT. UT WISI ENIM AD MINIM
VENIAM, QUIS NOSTRUD EXERCI TATION
ULLAMCORPER SUSCIPIT LOBORTIS NISL UT
ALIQUIP EX EA COMMODO CONSEQUAT. DUIS AUTEM

TYPE NB 55MS
TYPEDESIGN NEUBAU / STEFAN GANDL
DISTRIBURTOR WWW.NEUBAULADEN.COM

2002

[16

ABCDEFGHIJKLMNOPQRSTUVWXYZ
0123456789-(.,:?+!) «€» [/]&ß<>

[T

The *Neubau 55 Arabic Edition* by the designer Shaharzad
Khan is an adaptation of Stefan Gandl's roman face
Neubau 55. Gandl himself suggested he should do this. A
modern Arabic variant of this very austere typeface by
Gandl was produced by a laborious process – giving
due consideration to the basic framework of speech- and
connotation-determined Arabic script.

[120

[140

TYPE NB 55AL (ARABIC EDITION)
TYPEDESIGN SHAHARZAD KHAN OF MULE INDUSTRY (FOR NEUBAU)
DISTRIBURTOR WWW.NEUBAULADEN.COM

2004

[18

إإأإآآإ ابب يبيبتت تةطططت تجججج
حح خخ دددذ ///رزس سش شش مم ضضم طططضع غنغي
فف قف كككككككككككك گگلللمم
ننن٩٩ةييؤةعصص ههو يييئئئيي OIHYEDVNP

[8 / 9.5

كككئ مككككلكككككي لمككئ، بكككككئكككك ككككمك
كك كككك، ككككككككئك ككك كككمكك كككك لككك كككلككككك
كككككلكك كككككل مككككككمك كلككككككككك لككككككئ
ككككككك مككككككك كككككككئككك ككككك ككككككك
ككككك كككككك كككلك كككك كككككككك
كككككلككك كككككككككككك ككككككك كككككككئ ككئككك

—
DESIGN   NEUBAU / STEFAN GANDL
TYPE   NB 55AL
TYPEDESIGN   SHAHARZAD KHAN (FOR NEUBAU)
PHOTO   NEUBAU / STEFAN GANDL

—
DESIGN   EKHORNFORSS / NON-FORMAT
TYPE   NB55
TYPEDESIGN   NEUBAU / STEFAN GANDL

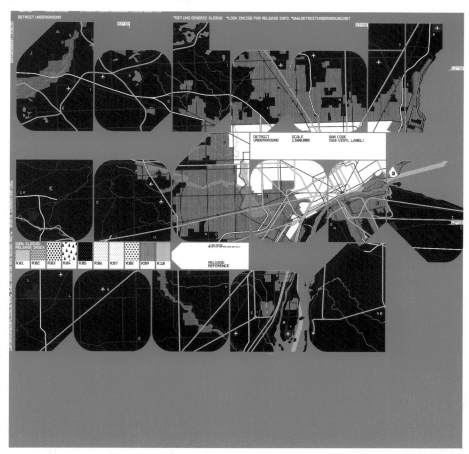

| TYPE | TM | 2003 |
| TYPEDESIGN | RICHARD NIESSEN | |

⌐ 20

ABCDEFGHIJKLMNOPQRSTUVWXYZ
abcdefghijklmnopqrstuvwxyz
0123456789

⌐ 120

⌐ 8 / 9.5

Lorem ipsum dolor sit amet, consectetuer adipiscing elit, sed diam nonummy nibh euismod tincidunt ut laoreet dolore magna aliquam erat volutpat. Ut wisi enim ad minim veniam, quis nostrud exerci tation ullamcorper suscipit lobortis nisl ut aliquip ex ea commodo consequat. Duis autem vel eum iriure dolor in hendrerit in vulputate velit esse molestie consequat, vel illum dolore eu feugiat nulla facilisis at vero et accumsan et iusto odio dignissim qui blandit praesent luptatum zzril delenit augue duis dolore te feugait nulla facilisi. Lorem ipsum dolor sit amet, consectetuer adipiscing elit, sed diam nonummy nibh euismod tincidunt ut laoreet dolore magna

---

| TYPE | CLOUD |
| TYPEDESIGN | FELLOW DESIGNERS |

⌐ 18

abcdefghijklm
nopqrstuvwxyzäåä

⌐ 72

| TYPE | VYNIL-BIG | 2001 |
| TYPEDESIGN | HAPPYPETS | |

⌐ 18

abcdefghijklmnopqrstuvwxyz
0123456789-.,?!'""

⌐ 72

Artis Ad de Jong en Jonas Ohlsson ABCD Slogan Mixed Interest Font Poster

---

TYPE ORIENT
TYPEDESIGN WOLFGANG ROSENTHAL
DISTRIBURTOR WWW.I-O-N.DE

1997

⌐ 14

⌐ 8 / 9.5

abcdefghijklmnopqrstuvwxyz
abcdefghijklmnopqrstuvwxyz
0123456789- .,:7 !

lorem ipsum dolor sit amet,
consectetuer adipiscing elit,
sed diam nonummy nibh
euismod tincidunt ut laoreet
dolore magna aliquam erat
volutpat. ut wisi enim ad
minim veniam, quis nostrud

TYPE FRAKTENDON
TYPEDESIGN LARS HARMSEN, BORIS KAHL
DISTRIBURTOR WWW.VOLCANO-TYPE.DE, WWW.MAGMA-KA.DE

2002

⌐ 18

⌐ 8 / 9.5

abcdefghijklmnopqrstuvwxyz
ABCDEFGHIJKLMNOPQRSTUVWXYZ
0123456789- .,:? !

Lorem ipsum dolor sit amet, consectetuer adipiscing
elit, sed diam nonummy nibh euismod tincidunt ut
laoreet dolore magna aliquam erat volutpat. Ut wisi
enim ad minim veniam, quis nostrud exerci tation
ullamcorper suscipit lobortis nisl ut aliquip ex ea
commodo consequat. Duis antem vel enm irinre dolor
in hendrerit in vulputate velit esse molestie

TYPE PLAYER SCRIPT
TYPEDESIGN ALEXANDER WISE

1999

⌐ 18

⌐ 72

abcdefghijklmnopqrstuvwxyz
ABCDEFGHIJKLMNOPQRSTUVWXYZ

smal

TYPE TARTAN BOLD
TYPEDESIGN RICHARD NIESSEN
DISTRIBURTOR FREE DOWNLOADABLE

2002

⌐ 18

⌐ 8 / 9.5

ABCDEFGHIJKLMNOPQRSTUVWXYZ
abcdefghijklmnopqrstuvwxyz
0123456789

Lorem ipsum dolor sit amet,
consectetuer adipiscing elit, sed
diam nonummy nibh euismod tincidunt
ut laoreet dolore magna aliquam erat
volutpat. Ut wisi enim ad minim
veniam, quis nostrud exerci tation
ullamcorper suscipit lobortis nisl ut

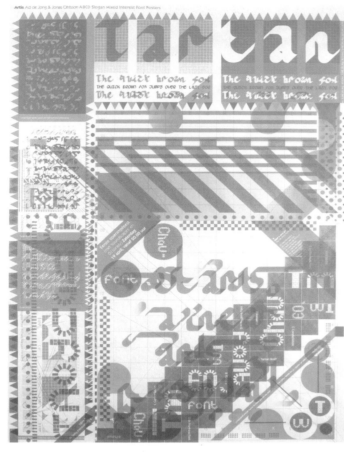

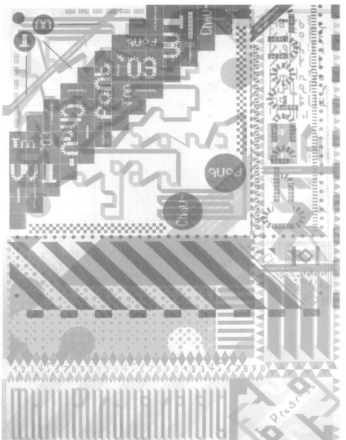

TYPE	SAMARKAND		2002
TYPEDESIGN	VITALIJ MEIER		
DISTRIBUTOR	I.S.K.R.A WERBEATELIER		

⌐ 18

⌐ T

Vitalij Meier's *Samarkand* typeface draws its strength from the dynamic typeface characteristics of the form, and from spirited calligraphy. The designer placed individual letters on top of each other or interwove them to produce an arabesque of ornamental typeface characteristics reminiscent of oriental, Indian or even Asiatic characters and ideograms. The designer pays homage to the richly textured history of the city of Samarkand in present-day Usbekistan.

⌐ 80

| TYPE | FLOMASTER-PLAIN | | 1998 |
| TYPEDESIGN | PFADFINDEREI, CRITZER / BBC BAD BOYS CREW, JAYONE | | |

⌐ 16

⌐ 8 / 9.5

Lorem ipsum dolor sit amet, consectetuer adipiscing elit, sed diam nonummy nibh euismod tincidunt ut laoreet dolore magna aliquam erat volutpat. Ut wisi enim ad minim veniam, quis nostrud exerci. Tation ullamcorper suscipit lobortis nisl, ut aliquip ex ea commodo consequat. Duis autem vel, eum iriure dolor in hendrerit in vulputate velit esse molestie consequat, vel illum dolore eu feugiat nulla facilisis at vero et accumsan et iusto odio dignissim qui blandit praesent luptatum zzril, delenit augue duis dolore te feugait nulla facilisi. Lorem ipsum dolor sit amet, consectetuer

⌐ 120

⌐ 120

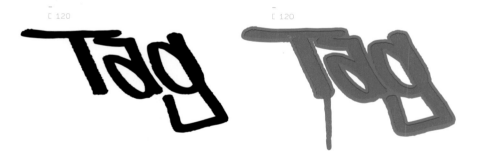

⌐ 12

FLOMASTER-PLAIN
FLOMASTER-FAT
FLOMASTER-OUTLINE
FLOMASTER-DROPS

- -

TYPE   131TRY-KLINSPOR
TYPEDESIGN   VIER5
DISTRIBUTOR   WWW.FORHOMEOROFFICEUSE.COM

2002

⌐ 18

ABCDEFGHIJKLMNOPQRSTUVWXYZ
abcdefghijklmnopqrstuvwxyz
0123456789-(.:;!) //(ex)

⌐ 8 / 9.5

Lorem ipsum dolor sit amet, consectetuer adipiscing elit,
sed diam nonummy nibh euismod tincidunt ut laoreet
dolore magna aliquam erat volutpat. Ut wisi enim ad
minim veniam, quis nostrud exerci tation ullamcorper
suscipit lobortis nisl ut aliquip ex ea commodo
consequat. Duis autem vel eum iriure dolor in hendrerit
in vulputate velit esse molestie consequat, vel illum

⌐ 72

⌐ 1

For the graphic designers of Vier5, typeface design
means both "drawing" and also creating tensions
between typefaces and other design resources. This
consistently leads to new, seemingly spontaneous,
expressive typeface forms.

- -

TYPE   161TRY-BITTER
TYPEDESIGN   VIER5
DISTRIBUTOR   WWW.FORHOMEOROFFICEUSE.COM

2001

⌐ 18

ABCDEFGHIJKLMNOPQRSTUVWXYZ
abcdefghijklmnopqrstuvwxyz
0123456789-(.:;+!) [/](ex)

⌐ 8 / 9.5

Lorem ipsum dolor sit amet, consectetuer adipiscing elit, sed
diam nonummy nibh euismod tincidunt ut laoreet dolore magna
aliquam erat volutpat. Ut wisi enim ad minim veniam, quis
nostrud exerci tation ullamcorper suscipit lobortis nisl ut
aliquip ex ea commodo consequat. Duis autem vel eum iriure
dolor in hendrerit in vulputate velit esse molestie consequat,
vel illum dolore eu feugiat nulla facilisis at vero et accumsan

- -

TYPE   ALMATADEMA EINS
TYPEDESIGN   VIER5
DISTRIBUTOR   WWW.FORHOMEOROFFICEUSE.COM

2003

⌐ 18

ABCDEFGHI /KLMND
PRRSTVVWXYZ
0 123456784

⌐ 72

- -

DESIGN   VIER5
TYPE   FT-BOLD, 18TRY-ANNETTE, LA BONNE HEURE
PHOTO   SUSAN HEBERT

FT

NEW BEAUTY

Rouge
letres
Dior

MISSO/UCCI

–
DESIGN   VIER5
TYPE   FT BOLD, 1TRY
PHOTO   JONAS UNGER, ROBIN SAUNDERS/MODELS1
–
PHOTO   ACHIM REICHERT, ANASTASIA/ADM

–
DESIGN   VIER5
TYPE   FT BOLD, 1TRY
PHOTO   JONAS UNGER, ROBIN SAUNDERS/MODELS1
–
PHOTO   ACHIM REICHERT, EMELINE/ADM

TYPE   0062APLOTTER ACHTUNDZWANZIG
TYPEDESIGN   VIER5
DISTRIBUTOR   WWW.FORHOMEOROFFICEUSE.COM

2003

[18

ABCDEFGHIJKLMNOPQRSTUVWXYZ
abcdefghijklmnopqrstuvwxyz
0 123456789 — (_,:?+!) «£» [/]&@<>

[8 / 9.5

Lorem ipsum dolor sit amet, consectetuer
adipiscing elit, sed diam nonummy nibh
euismod tincidunt ut laoreet dolore magna
aliquam erat volutpat. Ut wisi enim ad minim
veniam, quis nostrud exerci tation ullamcorper
suscipit lobortis nisl ut aliquip ex ea commodo
consequat. Duis autem vel eum iriure dolor in
hendrerit in vulputate velit esse molestie
consequat, vel illum dolore eu feugiat nulla
facilisis at vero et accumsan et iusto odio
dignissim qui blandit praesent luptatum zzril
delenit augue duis dolore te feugait nulla
facilisi. Lorem ipsum dolor sit amet,
consectetuer adipiscing elit, sed diam nonummy
nibh euismod tincidunt ut laoreet dolore magna
aliquam erat volutpat. Ut wisi enim ad minim
veniam, quis nostrud exerci tation ullamcorper
suscipit lobortis nisl ut aliquip ex ea commodo

[112

1z w e i

TYPE   025APLOTTER FUENFZIG
TYPEDESIGN   VIER5
DISTRIBUTOR   WWW.FORHOMEOROFFICEUSE.COM

2003

[20

ABCDEFGHIJKLMNOPQRSTUVWXYZ
abcdefghijklmnopqrstuvwxyz
0123456789—(_,:?+!) «£» [/]&@<>

[8 / 9.5

Lorem ipsum dolor sit amet, consectetuer adipiscing
elit, sed diam nonummy nibh euismod tincidunt ut
laoreet dolore magna aliquam erat volutpat. Ut wisi
enim ad minim veniam, quis nostrud exerci tation
ullamcorper suscipit lobortis nisl ut aliquip ex ea
commodo consequat. Duis autem vel eum iriure dolor
in hendrerit in vulputate velit esse molestie consequat,

[12

Plotter025a—Bandzug
025aPlotter Fuenfzig

[96

paste

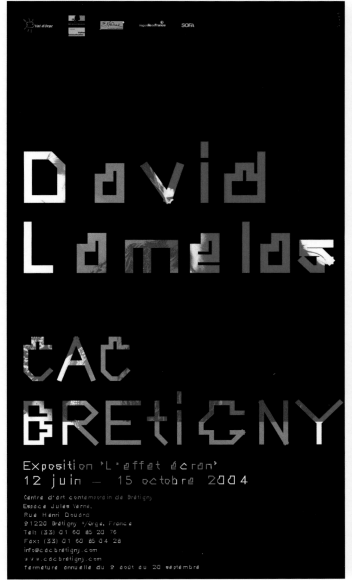

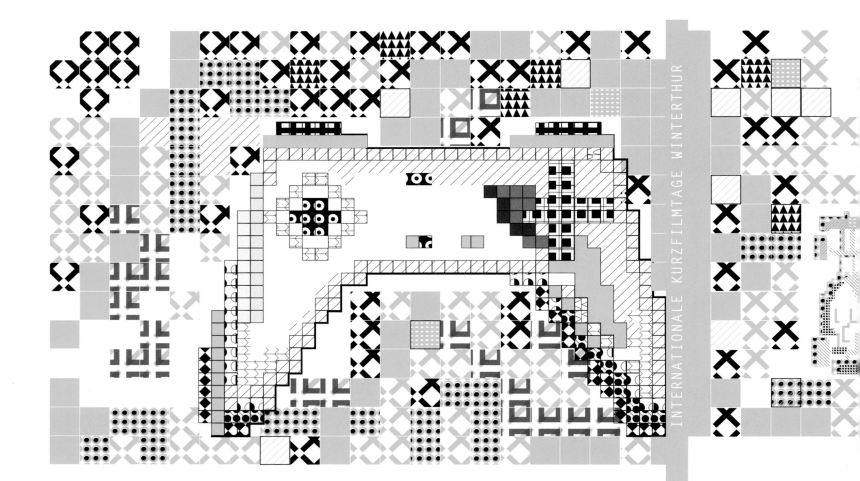

INTERNATIONALE KURZFILMTAGE WINTERTHUR

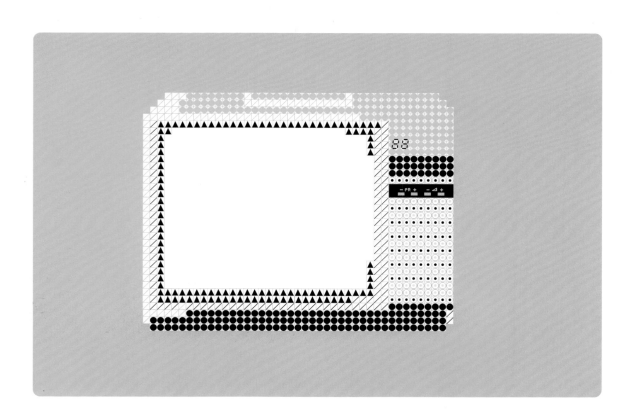

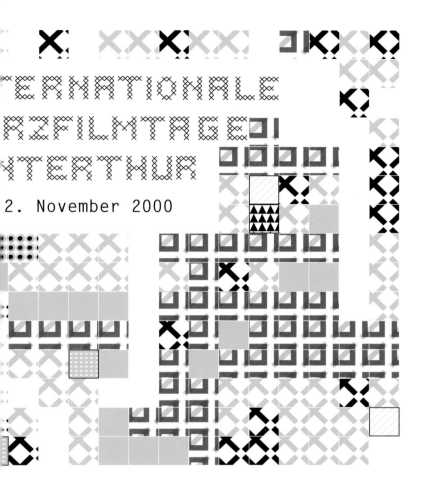

ERNATIONALE
RZFILMTAGE
NTERTHUR

2. November 2000

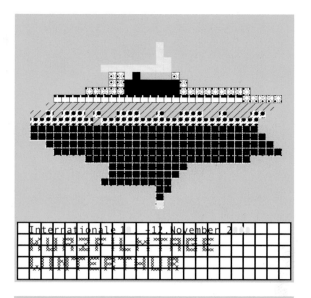

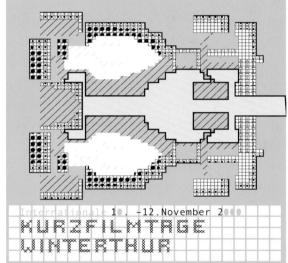

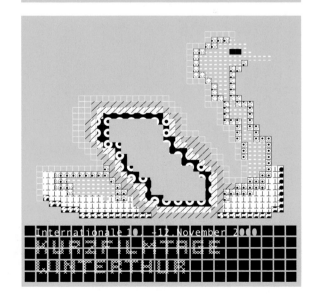

TYPE   ATARI
TYPEDESIGN   HAPPYPETS

2001

[18

ABCDEFGHIJKLMNOPQRSTUVWXYZ
abcdefghijklmnopqrstuvwxyz
0123456789-(,;:?+!)* ‹‹$›› ∫@▢_‹=›

[8 / 9.5

Lorem ipsum dolor sit amet, consectetuer adipiscing elit, sed diam nonummy nibh euismod tincidunt ut laoreet dolore magna aliquam erat volutpat. Ut wisi enim ad minim veniam, quis nostrud exerci tation ullamcorper suscipit lobortis nisl ut aliquip ex ea commodo consequat. Duis autem vel eum iriure dolor in hendrerit in vulputate

---

TYPE   PICHO
TYPEDESIGN   HAPPYPETS

1999

[18

abcdefghijklmnopqrstuvwxyz
0123456789-èéàôúö.,?! ▦ ▦ ▦ ▦▦▦
▦ ▦ ▦ ▦▦ ▦▦▦▦ ▦ ▦ ▦ ▦ ▦ ▦ ▦▦ ▦ ▦▦

[8 / 9.5

Lorem ipsum dolor sit amet, consectetuer adipiscing elit, sed diam nonummy nibh euismod tincidunt ut laoreet dolore magna aliquam erat volutpat. Ut wisi enim ad minim veniam, quis nostrud exerci tation ullamcorper suscipit lobortis nisl ut

[96

[12

picho-light
picho-regular
picho-bold

TYPE   MANIACAL-VER2.0
TYPEDESIGN   MASAYUKI SATO & JUNYA YAMADA
DISTRIBUTOR   MANIACKERS DESIGN / WWW.MKS.JP.ORG

2004

[16

ABCDEFGHIJKLMNOPQRSTUVWXYZ
abcdefghijklmnopqrstuvwxyz
0123456789-(,;:?·!)·/·&@

[8 / 9.5

Lorem ipsum dolor sit amet, consectetuer adipiscing elit, sed diam nonummy nibh euismod tincidunt ut laoreet dolore magna aliquam erat volutpat. Ut wisi enim ad minim veniam, quis nostrud exerci tation ullamcorper

---

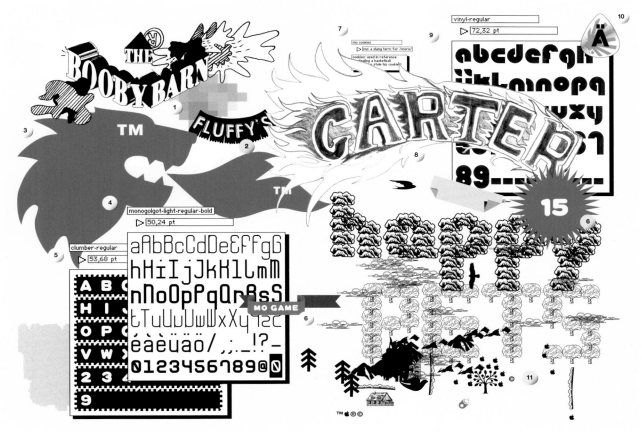

TYPE   AFK FONT   2003
TYPEDESIGN   RICHARD NIESSEN

⌐ 18   ⌐ 72

ɒuɔɔꝑꞔɐoɴ ɟɐʞʟⱱꞔoꝓoꞔꞔʇꞔꞔꞔʞɏɀ
0123456789

TYPE   IN PROGRESS   2003
TYPEDESIGN   RICHARD NIESSEN
DISTRIBUTOR   FREE DOWNLOADABLE

⌐ 16   ⌐ 8 / 9.5

ABCDEFGHIJKLMNOPQRSTU VWXYZ
abcdefghijkl mno pq rstu vwxyz
0123456789

Lorem ipsum dolor sit amet,
consectetuer adipiscing elit,
sed diam nonummy nibh euismod
tincidunt ut laoreet dolore
magna aliquam erat volutpat. Ut
wisi enim ad minim veniam, quis
nostrud exerci tation

TYPE   CONSTELLATION   2003
TYPEDESIGN   RICHARD NIESSEN
DISTRIBUTOR   FREE DOWNLOADABLE

⌐ 12   ⌐ 48

ABCDEFGHIJKLMNOPQRSTUVWXYZ
abcdefghijklmnopqrstuvwxyz
0123456789

TYPE   GOLDFINGER   1999
TYPEDESIGN   HAPPYPETS

⌐ 18   ⌐ 8 / 9.5

ABCDEFGHIJKLMNOPQRSTUVWXYZ
abcdefghijklmnopqrstuvwxyz
0123456789. ,;?!) g =

Lorem ipsum dolor sit amet, consectetuer
adipiscing elit, sed diam nonummy nibh euismod
tincidunt ut laoreet dolore magna aliquam erat
volutpat. Ut wisi enim ad minim veniam, quis
nostrud exerci tation ullamcorper suscipit lobortis
nisl ut aliquip ex ea commodo consequat. Duis
autem vel eum iriure dolor in hendrerit in

Wie is de held, wie is de anti-held?

Hommage aan Edgar Cairo

Hoe doorbreek je een taboe?

"Toen ik zelf met een Turkse vrouw trouwde, ben ik de zaken wel anders gaan zien."

Non-stop-black-rebel-music

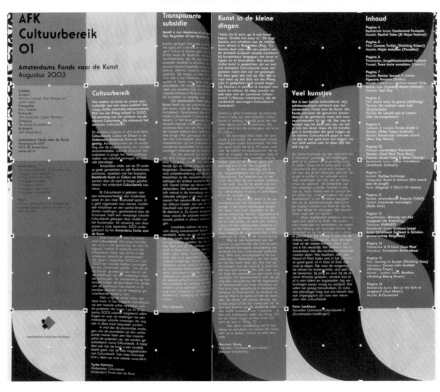

AFK Cultuurbereik 01

Amsterdams Fonds voor de Kunst
Augustus 2003

Transparante subsidie

Kunst in de kleine dingen

Inhoud

TYPE   LA BIRINTE   2003
TYPEDESIGN   ATELIER TÉLESCOPIQUE / XAVIER MEURICE
DISTRIBUTOR   FONDERIE NORDIK / WWW.ATELIERTELESCOPIQUE.COM

[22

ABCDEFGHIJKLMNOPQRSTUVWXYZ
abcdefghijklmnopqrstuvwxyz
0123456789-(.,:?*!)«»[/]&

[96

bonne

[8 / 9.5

Lorem ipsum dolor sit amet, consectetuer adipiscing elit. Sed diam nonummy nibh euismod tincidunt ut laoreet dolore magna aliquam erat volutpat. Ut wisi enim ad minim veniam, quis nostrud exerci tation ullamcorper suscipit lobortis nisl ut aliquip ex ea commodo consequat. Duis autem vel eum iriure dolor in hendrerit in vulputate velit esse molestie consequat, vel illum dolore eu feugiat nulla facilisis at vero et accumsan et iusto odio dignissim qui blandit praesent luptatum zzril delenit augue duis dolore te feugait nulla facilisi. Lorem ipsum dolor sit amet, consectetuer adipiscing elit. Sed diam nonummy nibh euismod tincidunt ut laoreet dolore magna aliquam erat volutpat. Ut wisi enim ad minim veniam, quis nostrud exerci

----

TYPE   ARVORE-OUTONO   2004
TYPEDESIGN   A' / CLARISSA TOSSIN
DISTRIBUTOR   WWW.DIE-GESTALTEN.DE

[18

• •
àâccefcñúxlmmopqrstuvwxyz
0123456789

[8 / 9.5

Lorem ipsum color sit amet, consectetuer adipiscing elit, sed diam nonummy nibh euismod tincidunt ut laoreet dolore magna aliquam erat volutpat. Ut wisi enim ad minim veniam, quis nostrud exerci tation ullamcorper suscipit lobortis nisl ut aliquip ex ea commodo consequat

[8 / 9.5

Arvore inverno
Arvore verão
Arvore outono
Arvore primavera

[36   [36

arvore   arvore

DESIGN   ATELIER TÉLESCOPIQUE
TYPE   LA BIRINTE
PHOTO   ATELIER TÉLESCOPIQUE

ch'est fait
à l'grosse mordake,
ch'est d'louvrache
ed pourchau.

www.
ateliertelescopique
com
Fonderie
nordik
rondie
download mac
free
for non
commercial
use
@ atelier
telescopique 98-04

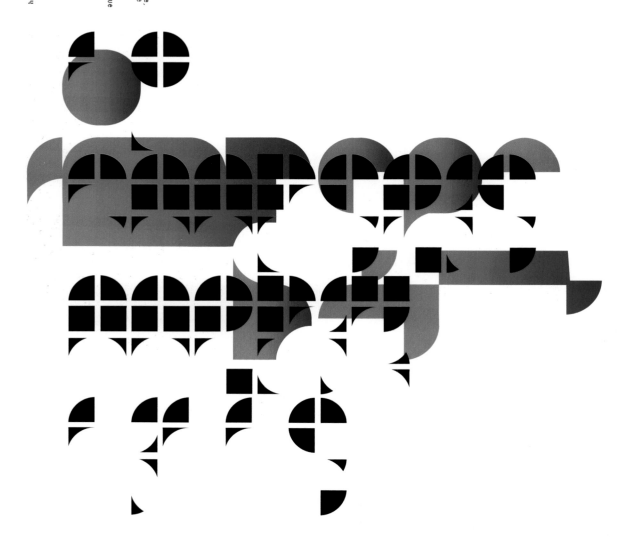

—
DESIGN   EKHORNFORSS / NON-FORMAT
TYPE   DS PLATTENBAU
TYPEDESIGNER   NEUBAU / STEFAN GANDL

TYPE   BDR MONO
TYPEDESIGN   BÜRO_DESTRUCT
DISTRIBUTOR   WWW.TYPEDIFFERENT.COM

1999

⌐ 14

ABCDEFGHIJKLMNOPQRSTUVWXYZ
ABCDEFGHIJKLMNOPQRSTUVWXYZ
0123456789
-(.,:?+!#)*«$£/.»[/]&∂□<=>

⌐ 58

⌐ 8 / 9.5

LOREM IPSUM DOLOR SIT AMET,
CONSECTETUER ADIPISCING ELIT. SED
DIAM NONUMMY NIBH EUISMOD
TINCIDUNT UT LAOREET DOLORE MAGNA
ALIQUAM ERAT VOLUTPAT. UT WISI
ENIM AD MINIM VENIAM, QUIS
NOSTRUD EXERCI TATION ULLAMCORPER
SUSCIPIT LOBORTIS NISL UT ALIQUIP
EX EA COMMODO CONSEQUAT. DUIS
AUTEM VEL EUM IRIURE DOLOR IN
HENDRERIT IN VULPUTATE VELIT ESSE
MOLESTIE CONSEQUAT, VEL ILLUM
DOLORE EU FEUGIAT NULLA FACILISIS
AT VERO ET ACCUMSAN ET IUSTO ODIO
DIGNISSIM QUI BLANDIT PRAESENT
LUPTATUM ZZRIL DELENIT AUGUE DUIS
DOLORE TE FEUGAIT NULLA FACILISI.
LOREM IPSUM DOLOR SIT AMET.

ZAPPING

TYPE   USSR
TYPEDESIGN   POWER GRAPHIXX

2001

⌐ 26

ABCDEFGHIJKLMNOPQRSTUVWXYZ
ABCDEFGHIJKLMNOPQRSTUVWXYZ
0123456789.,?!

⌐ 8 / 9.5

TYPE   AT TABAK
TYPEDESIGN   ATTAK / PETER KORSMAN
DISTRIBUTOR   WWW.ATTAKWEB.COM

2004

⌐ 16

ABCDEFGHIJKLMNOPQRSTUVWXYZ
0123456789-[.,:?+!] [/]+@↔

⌐ 8 / 9.5

LOREM IPSUM DOLOR SIT AMET,
CONSECTETUER ADIPISCING ELIT. SED
DIAM NONUMMY NIBH EUISMOD TINCIDUNT
UT LAOREET DOLORE MAGNA ALIQUAM ERAT
VOLUTPAT. UT WISI ENIM AD MINIM
VENIAM, QUIS NOSTRUD EXERCI TATION
ULLAMCORPER SUSCIPIT LOBORTIS NISL

DESIGN   BÜRO DESTRUCT
TYPE   BDR MONO

DESIGN   SLANGINTERNATIONAL.ORG
TYPE   HEAVY SKI RESORT

DESIGN   POWER GRAPHIXX
TYPE   USSR

DESIGN   ATTAK / PETER KORSMAN, CASPER HERSELMAN
TYPE   AT TABAK

DESIGN   BÜRO DESTRUCT
TYPE   BDR MONO

DESIGN   SLANGINTERNATIONAL.ORG
TYPE   HEAVY SKI RESORT

DESIGN   POWER GRAPHIXX
TYPE   USSR

DESIGN   ATTAK / PETER KORSMAN, CASPER HERSELMAN
TYPE   AT TABAK

TYPE   PICO-BLACK
TYPEDESIGN   MASAYUKI SATO
DISTRIBUTOR   MANIACKERS DESIGN / WWW.MKS.JP.ORG

—
2004

—
⌐ 18

—
⌐ 8 / 9.5

oabcdefghijklmnopqrstuvwxyz
abcdefghijklMnoPqrstuvwxYz
0123456789-(.,:?+!) ⌐ / J&@<>

lorem ipsum dolor sit amet, consectetuer
adipiscing elit, sed diam nonummy nibh
euismod tincidunt ut laoreet dolore magna
aliquam erat volutpat. ut wisi enim ad minim
veniam, quis nostrud exerci tation
ullamcorper suscipit lobortis nisl ut aliquip ex
ea commodo consequat. duis autem vel eum

TYPE   BUILDANDSCRAP
TYPEDESIGN   POWER GRAPHIXX

—
2001

—
⌐ 16

—
⌐ 96

ABCDEFGHIJKLMNOPQRSTUVWXYZ
ABCDEFGHIJKLMNOPQRSTUVWXYZ
0123456789

TYPE   LOGASMEN-LIGHT
TYPEDESIGN   PFADFINDEREI / MARTIN ALEITH
DISTRIBUTOR   WWW.DIE-GESTALTEN.DE

—
2003

—
⌐ 18

—
⌐ 8 / 9.5

abcdefghijklmnopqrstuvwxyz
ABCDEFGHIJKLMNOPQRSTUVWXYZ
0123456789-(.,?+!) «E» [/] &@←→

Lorem ipsum dolor sit amet,
consectetuer adipiscing elit, sed diam
nonummy nibh euismod tincidunt ut
laoreet dolore magna aliquam erat
volutpat. ut wisi enim ad minim veniam, quis
nostrud exerci tation ullamcorper
suscipit lobortis nisl ut aliquip ex ea

TYPE   WINTER
TYPEDESIGN   ALEXANDER WISE
DISTRIBUTOR   WWW.DIE-GESTALTEN.DE

—
2003

—
⌐ 12

—
⌐ 8 / 9.5

abcdefghijklmnopqrstuvwxyz
ABCDEFGHIJKLMNOPQRSTUVWXYZ
0123456789-(.,?+!) «E» [/] &@<>

Lorem ipsum dolor sit amet,
consectetuer adipiscing elit,
sed diam nonummy nibh
euismod tincidunt ut laoreet
dolore magna aliquam erat
volutpat. ut wisi enim ad minim
veniam, quis nostrud exerci

DESIGN   PFADFINDEREI / MARTIN ALEITH
TYPE   LOGASMEN

TYPE   MERICK
TYPEDESIGN   ATELIER TÉLESCOPIQUE / SÉBASTIEN DELOBEL   2003
DISTRIBUTOR   FONDERIE NORDIK / WWW.ATELIERTELESCOPIQUE.COM

◻ 12

ABCDEFGHIJKLMNOPQRSTUVWXYZ
abcdefghijklmnopqrstuvwxyz
@123456789-[.,:?+!] «£» [/]&@<>

◻ 8 / 9.5

Lorem ipsum dolor sit amet,
consectetuer adipiscing
elit, sed diam nonummy
nibh euismod tincidunt ut
laoreet dolore magna
aliquam erat volutpat. Ut
wisi enim ad minim veniam,
quis nostrud exerci tation
ullamcorper suscipit
lobortis nisl ut aliquip ex
ea commodo consequat. Duis
autem vel eum iriure dolor
in hendrerit in vulputate
velit esse molestie
consequat, vel illum dolore
eu feugiat nulla facilisis
at vero et accumsan et
iusto odio dignissim qui

◻ 48

kiosque

TYPE   MONOGOLGOT
TYPEDESIGN   HAPPYPETS   1999

◻ 18

ABCDEFGHIJKLMNOPQRSTUVWXYZ
abcdefghijklmnopqrstuvwxyz
0123456789-[.,:;?!)˜˝/@_éèàäüö

◻ 12

Monogolgot-Light

Monogolgot-Regular

Monogolgot-Bold

TYPE   CA LOVECHAIR-PLUTO
TYPEDESIGN   STEFAN CLAUDIUS   2003
DISTRIBUTOR   CAPE ARCONA TYPE FOUNDRY / WWW.CAPE-ARCONA.COM

◻ 20

ABCDEFGHIJKLMNOPQRSTUVWXYZ
abcdefghijklmnopqrstuvwxyz
0123456789-(.,:?+!#)* «$£%» [/]&@ß<=>

◻ 8 / 9.5

Lorem ipsum dolor sit amet, consectetuer adipiscing elit, sed diam
nonummy nibh euismod tincidunt ut laoreet dolore magna aliquam
erat volutpat. Ut wisi enim ad minim veniam, quis nostrud exerci
tation ullamcorper suscipit lobortis nisl ut aliquip ex ea commodo
consequat. Duis autem vel eum iriure dolor in hendrerit in vulputate
velit esse molestie consequat, vel illum dolore eu feugiat nulla

---

ch'est fait
à l'grosse mordake,
ch'est q'iouvrache
ed pourchau.

www
ateliertelescopique
.com
fonderie
nordik
merick

© atelier
telescopique 98-04

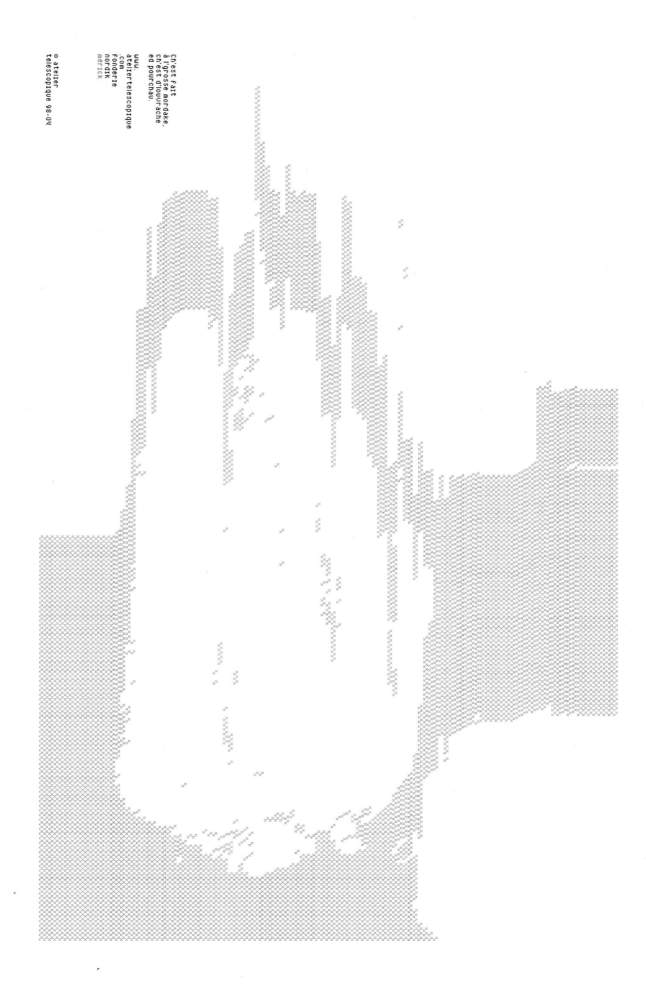

TYPE   KADA
TYPEDESIGN JOEL NORDSTRÖM
DISTRIBUTOR WWW.LINETO.COM

2002

18

ABCDEFGHIJKLMNOPQRSTUVWXYZ
ABCDEFGHIJKLMNOPQRSTUVWXYZ
0123456789-(.,:?+!#)* «$£%» [/]&@$$<=>

8 / 9.5

LOREM IPSUM DOLOR SIT AMET,
CONSECTETUER ADIPISCING ELIT, SED
DIAM NONUMMY NIBH EUISMOD TINCIDUNT
UT LAOREET DOLORE MAGNA ALIQUAM
ERAT VOLUTPAT. UT WISI ENIM AD MINIM
VENIAM, QUIS NOSTRUD EXERCI TATION
ULLAMCORPER SUSCIPIT LOBORTIS NISL
UT ALIQUIP EX EA COMMODO CONSEQUAT.
DUIS AUTEM VEL EUM IRIURE DOLOR IN
HENDRERIT IN VULPUTATE VELIT ESSE
MOLESTIE CONSEQUAT, VEL ILLUM
DOLORE EU FEUGIAT NULLA FACILISIS AT
VERO ET ACCUMSAN ET IUSTO ODIO
DIGNISSIM QUI BLANDIT PRAESENT
LUPTATUM ZZRIL DELENIT AUGUE DUIS
DOLORE TE FEUGAIT NULLA FACILISI.
LOREM IPSUM DOLOR SIT AMET,
CONSECTETUER ADIPISCING ELIT. SED

170

TYPE   DOOR TO DOOR
TYPEDESIGN MARTIN WOODTLI

1999

14

ABCDEFGHIJKLMNOPQRSTUVWXYZ
0123456789 Q

72

TYPE   HANDGUN
TYPEDESIGN HANDGUN / DAVID ZACK CUSTER

2004

16

ABCDEFGHIJKLMNOPQRSTUVWXYZ
0123456789

72

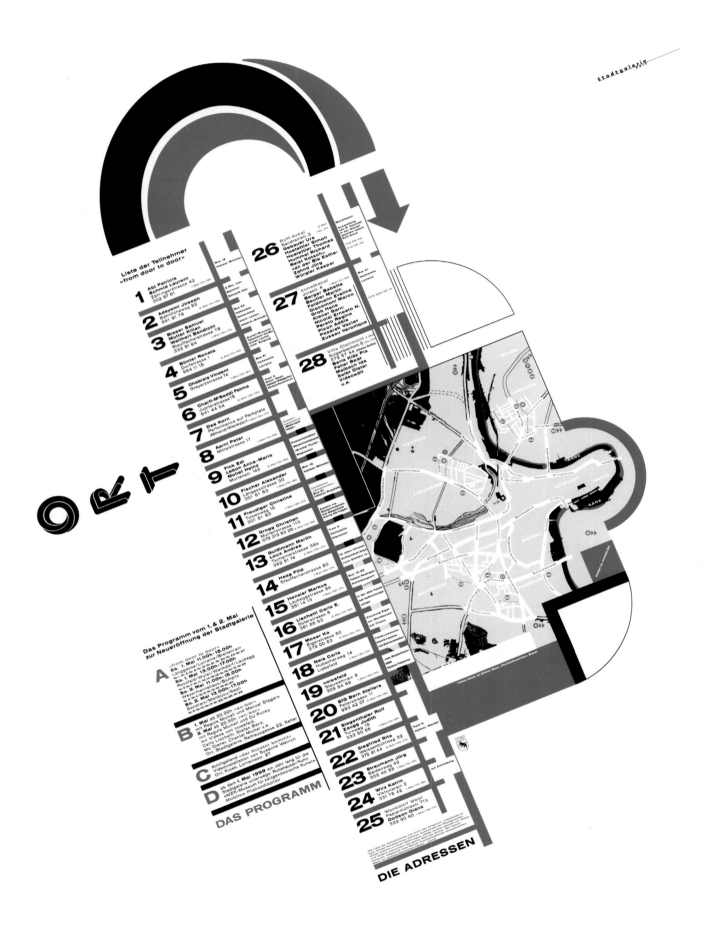

DESIGN MOIRÉ. MARC KAPPELER
TYPEDESIGN MARC KAPPELER
ILLUSTRATION BENJAMIN GÜDEL

CHF 28.- magazine for mental lifestyle
EUR 25.- www.soDA.ch
USD 26.-

9 771424 671008

TYPE   CARGO
TYPEDESIGN   GAVILLET & RUST
DISTRIBUTOR   WWW.OPTIMO.CH

2002

⌐ 18

ABCDEFGHIJKLMNOPQRSTUVWXYZ
abcdefghijklmnopqrstuvwxyz
0123456789-[.,:?+!#]* «$£%» [/]&@ß<=>

⌐ T

Stencil type was originally used to transfer a text or individual letters in ink onto rough material, or material that was difficult to print on. This meant that the outlines of the letters were seldom sharp. Another typical feature of stencil type is formally significant horizontal or diagonal interventions intended to stop the counters breaking away. Optimo's *Cargo* typeface deliberately uses this technically determined inadequacy as a design device. First applications as a creative expressive device appeared in the early 1920s. Even the Bauhaus artist Josef Albers constructed letters from geometrical shapes that were interrupted at certain points.

⌐ 96   ⌐ 96

EIN ein

TYPE   MONTANA
TYPEDESIGN   GAVILLET & RUST
DISTRIBUTOR   WWW.OPTIMO.CH

2003

⌐ 16

ABCDEFGHIJKLMNOPQRSTUVWXYZ
abcdefghijklmnopqrstuvwxyz
0123456789-[.,:?+!#]* «$£%» [/]&@ß<=>

⌐ 8 / 9.5

Lorem ipsum dolor sit amet, consectetuer adipiscing elit, sed diam nonummy nibh euismod tincidunt ut laoreet dolore magna aliquam erat volutpat. Ut wisi enim ad minim veniam, quis nostrud exerci tation ullamcorper suscipit lobortis nisl ut aliquip ex ea commodo consequat. Duis autem vel eum iriure dolor

⌐ 96   ⌐ 96

AUS aus

⌐ 12

Montana-Light
Montana-Regular
Montana-Bold

TYPE KIT-FAT 1999
TYPEDESIGN ERIK JOHAN WORSØE ERIKSEN
DISTRIBUTOR WWW.DIE-GESTALTEN.DE

_ 18

ABCDEFGHIJKLMNOPQRSTUVWXYZ
abcdefghijklmnopqrstuvwxyz
0123456789-(.,:?+!) «£» (/)&@<>

_ 72

_ 8 / 9.5

Lorem ipsum dolor sit amet, consectetuer adipiscing elit, sed diam nonummy nibh euismod tincidunt ut laoreet dolore magna aliquam erat volutpat. Ut wisi enim ad minim veniam, quis nostrud exerci tation ullamcorper suscipit lobortis nisl ut aliquip ex ea commodo consequat. Duis autem vel eum iriure dolor in hendrerit in vulputate velit esse molestie consequat, vel illum dolore eu feugiat nulla facilisis at vero et accumsan et iusto odio dignissim qui blandit praesent luptatum zzril delenit augue duis dolore te feugait nulla facilisi. Lorem ipsum dolor sit amet, consectetuer adipiscing elit, sed diam nonummy nibh euismod tincidunt ut laoreet dolore magna aliquam erat volutpat. Ut wisi enim ad minim veniam, quis nostrud exerci tation ullamcorper suscipit lobortis nisl ut aliquip ex ea commodo consequat. Duis autem

---

TYPE RHODESIA-BLACK 2003
TYPEDESIGN NORM

_ 16

ABCDEFGHIJKLMNOPQRSTUVWXYZ
abcdefghijklmnopqrstuvwxyz
0123456789-(.,:?+!) «£» [/]&@<>

_ 8 / 9.5

Lorem ipsum dolor sit amet, consectetuer adipiscing elit, sed diam nonummy nibh euismod tincidunt ut laoreet dolore magna aliquam erat volutpat. Ut wisi enim ad minim veniam, quis nostrud exerci tation ullamcorper suscipit lobortis nisl ut aliquip ex ea commodo consequat. Duis autem vel eum iriure dolor in hendrerit in vulputate

---

TYPE RHODESIA-SUPERBLACK ROUNDED 2003
TYPEDESIGN NORM

_ 16

ABCDEFGHIJKLMNOPQRSTUVWXYZ
0123456789-(.,:?+!) «£» [/]&@<>

_ 12

Rhodesia-Black Rounded

RHODESIA-SUPERBLACK

TYPE HARDCASE
TYPEDESIGN DMITRI LAVROW
DISTRIBUTOR WWW.FONTSHOP.DE

1997

[14 HARDCASE HARDCASE-45LIGHT

ABCDEFGHIJKLMNOPQRSTUVWXYZ
abcdefghijklmnopqrstuvwxyz
◊123456789-
(.,:?+!#)*«$£%»[/]&@ß<=>

[8 / 9.5

Lorem ipsum dolor sit amet, consectetuer adipiscing elit, sed diam nonummy nibh euismod tincidunt ut laoreet dolore magna aliquam erat volutpat. Ut wisi enim ad minim veniam, quis nostrud exerci tation ullamcorper suscipit lobortis nisl ut aliquip ex ea commodo consequat. Duis autem vel eum iriure dolor in hendrerit in vulputate velit esse molestie consequat, vel illum dolore eu feugiat nulla facilisis at vero et

[9

HardCase-25UltraLight
HardCase-45Light
HardCase-65DemiBold
HardCase-47LightCondensed

[9

HardCase-951Stencil
HardCase-955Cameo
HardCase-422Bad
HardCase-410Dotted

TYPE EXECUTIVE CEO
TYPEDESIGN FRANÇOIS RAPPO
DISTRIBUTOR WWW.ÖPTIMO.CH

2004

[16

ABCDEFGHIJKLMNOPQRSTUVWXYZ
abcdefghijklmnopqrstuvwxyz
0123456789
-(.,:?+!#)*«$£%»[/]&@ß<=>

[8 / 9.5

Lorem ipsum dolor sit amet, consectetuer adipiscing elit, sed diam nonummy nibh euismod tincidunt ut laoreet dolore magna aliquam erat volutpat. Ut wisi enim ad minim veniam, quis nostrud exerci tation ullamcorper suscipit

[60

account

[12

ExecutiveCEO-Medium
ExecutiveCEO-Bold

AUTUNNO | INVERNO
1999 | 2000

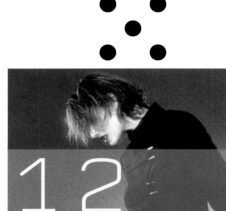

12

MODELLO		COMPOSIZIONE	
GIACCA	ARTICOLO 7029 9302	95%WV	LANA VERGINE
JOSI B.		5%PA	POLIAMIDE
PANTALONE	ARTICOLO 4029 4704	95%WV	LANA VERGINE
HESTER D.		5%PA	POLIAMIDE

AUTUNNO | INVERNO
1999 | 2000

04

MODELLO		COMPOSIZIONE	
CAPPOTTO	ARTICOLO 6029 6702	70%WV	LANA VERGINE
MELANIE B.		20%PA	POLIAMIDE
		10%WM	MOHAIR
PANTALONE	ARTICOLO 4029 4504	60%VI	VISCOSA
HELLA D.		37%PL	POLIESTERE
		3%EA	ELASTANE

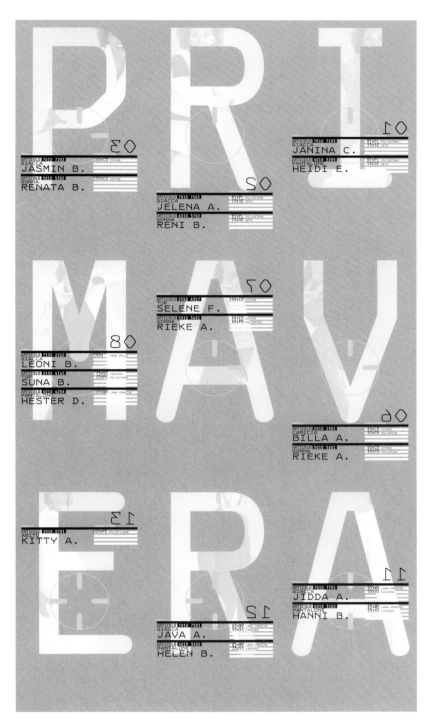

PRI MAV ERA

03
ARTICOLO 7010 7202	100%CO COTONE
GIACCA	
JASMIN B.	
ARTICOLO 5010 5502	100%CO COTONE
GONNA	
RENATA B.	

01
ARTICOLO 7010 7101	81%PL POLIESTERE
GIACCA	19%SE SETA
JANINA C.	
ARTICOLO 4010 3205	81%PL POLIESTERE
PANTALONE	19%SE SETA
HEIDI E.	

02
ARTICOLO 7010 7501	81%PL POLIESTERE
GIACCA	19%SE SETA
JELENA A.	
ARTICOLO 4010 3702	81%PL POLIESTERE
GONNA	19%SE SETA
RENI B.	

05
ARTICOLO 2550 6357	100%CO COTONE
TOP	
SELENE F.	
ARTICOLO 5010 5601	60%CO COTONE
GONNA	40%PA POLIAMIDE
RIEKE A.	

08
ARTICOLO 7350 2262	100% VERA PELLE
GIACCA	
LEONI B.	
ARTICOLO 2550 6165	77%VI VISCOSA
TOP	23%PL POLIESTERE
SUNA B.	
ARTICOLO 4010 3204	100%WV LANA VERGINE
PANTALONE	
HESTER D.	

06
ARTICOLO 2010 1001	52%CO COTONE
CAMICIA	48%PA POLIAMIDE
BILLA A.	
ARTICOLO 5010 5601	60%PA POLIAMIDE
GONNA	40%PA POLIAMIDE
RIEKE A.	

13
ARTICOLO 1010 0701	100%PL POLIESTERE
ABITO	
KITTY A.	

11
ARTICOLO 7010 7201	64%WV LANA VERGINE
GIACCA	36%VI VISCOSA
JIDDA A.	
ARTICOLO 4010 3502	64%WV LANA VERGINE
PANTALONE	36%VI VISCOSA
HANNI B.	

12
ARTICOLO 7010 7601	65%WV LANA VERGINE
GIACCA	35%VI VISCOSA
JAVA A.	
ARTICOLO 4010 3502	65%WV LANA VERGINE
PANTALONE	35%VI VISCOSA
HELEN B.	

TYPE AMATEUR
TYPEDESIGN BONBON / VALERIA BONIN, DIEGO BONTOGNALI
DISTRIBUTOR BONBON

2003

⌐ 14

⌐ 8 / 9.5

ABCDEFGHIJKLMNOPQRSTUVWXYZ
abcdefghijklmnopqrstuvwxyz
0123456789-
(. , : ? + ! →) ˣ « $? % » [/] & @ ß ‹ = ›

Lorem ipsum dolor sit amet,
consectetuer adipiscing elit, sed
diam nonummy nibh euismod tincidunt
ut laoreet dolore magna aliquam erat
volutpat. Ut wisi enim ad minim
veniam, quis nostrud exerci tation
ullamcorper suscipit lobortis nisl ut

TYPE NACONDA
TYPEDESIGN ATELIER TÉLESCOPIQUE / XAVIER MEURICE
DISTRIBUTOR FONDERIE NORDIK / WWW.ATELIERTELESCOPIQUE.COM

2004

⌐ 16

⌐ 8 / 9.5

ABCDEFGHIJKLMNOPQRSTUVWXYZ
abcdefghijklmnopqrstuvwxyz
0123456789-[.,:?+!#]*«$⋸%»[/]&@ß<=>

Lorem ipsum dolor sit amet, consectetuer
adipiscing elit, sed diam nonummy nibh
euismod tincidunt ut laoreet dolore magna
aliquam erat volutpat. Ut wisi enim ad
minim veniam, quis nostrud exerci tation
ullamcorper suscipit lobortis nisl ut aliquip

⌐ 96

⌐ 12

Naconda-Light
Naconda-Regular
Naconda-Italic
Naconda-Bold

TYPE TSTAR MONO ROUND
TYPEDESIGN MIKA MISCHLER
DISTRIBUTOR WWW.DIE-GESTALTEN.DE

2001

⌐ 16

⌐ 8 / 9.5

ABCDEFGHIJKLMNOPQRSTUVWXYZ
abcdefghijklmnopqrstuvwxyz
0123456789-
[. , : ? + ! #] * « $£%» [/]&@ß<=>

Lorem ipsum dolor sit amet,
consectetuer adipiscing elit, sed
diam nonummy nibh euismod tincidunt
ut laoreet dolore magna aliquam erat
volutpat. Ut wisi enim ad minim
veniam, quis nostrud exerci tation
ullamcorper suscipit lobortis nisl

DESIGN   NICOLAS BOURQUIN
PHOTO   PIET TRUHLAR
TYPE   TSTAR MONO ROUND
TYPEDESIGN   MIKA MISCHLER

En faveur de "Insieme Cerebral du Jura bernois", Tavannes

Triathlon Populaire
Piscine du Château
Tramelan
samedi 16 août 2003

programme

triathlon jeunesse
9.30 - 10.00 h: inscription
10.30 h: départ

triathlon populaire
9.30 - 12.30 h: inscription
12.30 h: dossards
14.00 h: départ

disciplines

individuel:
natation 200 m
VTT 10 km
course à pied 4 km

équipes:
natation 300 m
VTT 10 km
course à pied 4 km

categories

écoliers,écolieres 1991-1993
équipe
50 m/1,5 km/1 km

cadets, cadettes 1988-1990
équipe
100 m/3 km/2 km

dames 1: 1978 - 1989
dames 2: 1977 et -
hommes 1: 1973 - 1989
hommes 2: 1972 et -
équipe: 2-3 pers. dès 14 ans

organisation

paroisse réformée, Tramelan
www.paroisse-tramelan.ch

délai d'insription: 12.8.2003
triathlon@paroisse-tramelan.ch
tél. 032 487 62 84

affiche: Nicolas Bourquin
photo: Piet Truhlar
modèle: Anja
font: Mika Mischler

TITLE   MY FACE OR YOURS?
AUTHOR   FRANÇOIS RAPPO
CHARACTERS   16.487

In our digital age, the language of modern typography keeps turning unexpectedly to the past. Although the term "fonderie" (type foundry)[1] is an ironic metaphor from a post-industrial point of view, relating to the mechanical production of fonts[2], it is still the best definition of the competencies needed for any typographical design.

The meaning of the word "fonderie" does more than simply evoke the image of an outdated industrial process. In fact it brings three competencies together: concept, production, distribution. These are functions that are almost unchanged today. But in the 1980s, type production finally detached itself from typesetting machines – the new term is "hardware". Until now, the interplay of specialised competencies (typeface design, visual balance, scaled reduction of designs to microtypographical textual requirements, to say nothing of the technologies associated with them) was supported by infrastructures that were sufficiently constraining and specific to function as a unit. Commercially speaking, type foundries were long-lived family businesses, regular dynasties in which both capital and skills acquired over the centuries were passed down through the generations. This applied to the Haas type foundry in Switzerland, for example, from 1740 to their last product, *Haas-Unica* in the 1980s, shortly before the business was discontinued as digital technology became more widespread.

Industrial type foundries in the old style lasted for a long time and also represented the geographical centre of a centralised distribution system. The degree of centralisation was in proportion with the link between the letters and the cost of the equipment needed to use them (look at the Monotype or Berthold type foundries which used to have a complete programme handling absolutely everything to do with setting type, and who influenced the design of large quantities of printed matter, just as software does today).

The "dematerialised" manufacture of letters that has prevailed since the 1990s is no longer hardware-driven. Does this mean that graphics and visual communication are now essentially random fields? "Next Wave", the standard typography discourse of the 1990s, has repeated this view like a mantra, and made it into a credo (see for example: *Typography now, the Next Wave* by Rick Poyner and Edward Booth-Clibborn, Booth-Clibborn Editions, London, 1991). Hence the question: what is typeface manufacture today? Is it something objective? Is it a network? Or a certain set of skills and competencies? An interface that brings various groups with different competencies together? And what are they? Forgetting about metaphors, what we need is a concept that will allow us to put concept, production and distribution together in a sustainable package of competencies. Dematerialisation = democratisation? The tools have democratised themselves: professional typeface creation software costs about $600. And you can put the question about democratisation in a different way: we have the ability to produce the lettering for a certain project as a complete font. Yes, democratisation has taken place, and it seems superfluous to argue about the boundaries between lettering and real typography. Otherwise we would have

to ask: what type of reading matter are we talking about – headlines, a book, an advertisement, a flyer, a railway timetable, online or on paper? As far as book typography is concerned, democratisation has not been complete. But there can't be any doubt that democratisation as a new feeling of "closeness" has set in among typography users, graphic designers, editors and publishers, in terms of the typefaces and alphabets on their PCs. Specialised users feel this closeness, as is to be expected, but so do the broad mass of typography users; you and me in our daily lives.

The "fonderie" label is reminiscent – deliberately, no doubt – in our modern service society of the industry's nostalgic past, as typographic production is a service now as well. An open range of services that is mobile by definition and extends from precisely definable items (lettering, custom types, corporate typeface) to a whole series of indeterminate values and products (consultancy, label-free typefaces that have a high symbolic and recognition value, self-publications etc.) A typographic product can now be an "attitude" as well. Here it should be emphasised that the values associated with these services are gender oriented. Is a passion for typographic design still an overwhelmingly male quality? Is this the price (or the tribute) that has to be paid to the outmoded capitalism of the industrial age type foundries? Or to the super-ego that was doubtless indispensable for the functioning of these family firms, which are generally presented as austere and abstemious?

So the type foundry links design, manufacture and sales. Designing and manufacturing characters now seem to be linked via digital tools. It is a very quick step from sketches made by various techniques to vectorisation, if you haven't been using a vector-oriented method in the first place. The production processes vary from one designer to the next. The programs are so flexible that no constraints of scale are imposed upon design. Production, i.e. publishing a font (mastering), is part of the process.

Manufacturing methods were gradually standardised: a kind of binding stereotype developed from the same programs and the same visual cultures towards the end of the 1970s. In the meantime, pretty well everyone has exhausted the possibilities offered by the current program tools: cut/copy/paste. Thus we are ready once again to look more complex formal problems in the eye. But the enthusiasm of past decades should not be suppressed at this new stage. The new designers, who have had digital access to typography from the start, and the exponents of older methods are coming together! And the typographical products they each make are starting to fuse! Precisely now, at the beginning of the 21st century, the visual culture of many digital type foundries seems to be lacking a pragmatic, functional element. Could it not also be that design and manufacture are too closely linked when they are directly linked in digital typography? Is it not the case that most digital typefaces look too "drawn", to much influenced by their large-scale appearance? Whether they are made in pencil or with vector tools, perhaps most typefaces are conceived too "visually" and not sufficiently "textually": they are hardly devised for the real graphic scale on which they are used and also can hardly cope with the mass of characters that have to be absorbed in large quantities. But this means that they were created without text in mind. The ability to maximise the density of the information contained in the text is an essential feature of typography – handwriting or comparable typefaces deliver less in this respect. Most of today's letters (including the ones that I risk making) seem to be conceived for use with a three- or four-centimetre "x-height". Is this something to do with the size in which they were designed? All these typefaces share a remarkable love of detail, whether they are "neo-neo-constructivist" or "historicist-revivalist". A style like this would be good for title pages or display versions[7]. But can these typefaces take massive graphic density? What about their "micrographic" value[8], which is a truly typographical quality.

It is hard to define the function-dependent, specific quality of textual letters; it can be about variations within a character set or a plain functional quality that resists the formal smoothing that digital, all too "macrographic" typography has to undergo. The fact that we can "flash" offset plates for CPT printing at almost 4,000 dpi does not help to solve the problem, it just makes it more acute.

We need a kind of – hypothetical – software that would help us to reconstruct the specific qualities of typographic design and to transfer this into the digital process. A start has been made on this in the writings of William Addison Dwiggins (*WAD to RR, a letter about designing type*, Cambridge, Harvard College Library, 1940), or recently in Fred Smeijeer's work (*Type Now*, Hyphen Press, London, 2003).

The specific quality of the micrographic presentation of a text can be recognised in design or in the gravure of letters designed by the old techniques to a font size of 12 points (1 Cicero in the *old-style* nomenclature). Their visual typology is entirely distinct from that of title letters devised by designers. The digital process should play closer heed to this distinction. But this should not be done too dogmatically, so that the visual possibilities can continue to remain so open and so complex that anyone can develop his own graphic culture.

One of the most interesting tendencies developing in typography today seems to me to be one based on questions in the fields of digital "type founding". This is a new stage. Is it possible to detect a kind of "Post-Next-Wave" of typeface creation (or even its return) in the work of some designers? Are we going back to the text, after the types "with attitude"? Back to typographic tasks that need more work on them? Above all, using new possibilities to translate the elements of traditional text-character micro-aesthetics into the digital sphere. The postmodern component of this approach, which goes beyond "historicism" (relying too much on the past) is captured fairly precisely in the concepts "poly-historical" and "synthetic", as developed by Andy Crewdson in his introduction to Peter Belak's *Fedra* specimen (*Fedra* specimen, Typoteque.com,

The Hague, 2003). This is how many contemporary designers, with all the variety of approaches they take, have worked out, explicitly and convincingly, the connection between digital graphic methods and historical typography. But what about a comparable re-examination of the Modernist tradition? Is there an "incomplete Modernism" in our field, as there could be said to be in architecture? Perhaps not, but a Modernism that has a real development potential. Here too it would make sense to think back to the historical sequence of modernistic products. For example the sans-serif faces[12], from the primitive Grotesques[11] of the 19th and early-20th centuries down to the ultra-smoothed fonts of the 1950s and the 1970s, from *Helvetica* to *Frutiger*. And we could also try to continue the sequence neo-Modernism, synthetic post-postmodernism, neo-Rationalism. All this is of course part of the type foundry of the future.

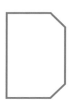

TITLE   MY FACE OR YOURS?
AUTHOR   FRANÇOIS RAPPO
CHARACTERS   16.487

1   Fonderie: originally a firm who made lead type that was cast in matrixes and/or the equipment that enabled type to be cast in the setting shops. Today the meaning has been metaphorically extended, and could still be applied to companies who make and sell typefaces.

2   Font (character set): a group of letters in the same style including upper- and lower-case letters, numbers and the necessary special characters. Originally a character set was restricted to a single size in lead typesetting. The old Postscript format includes 256 characters, OpenType can have several thousand characters. A group of faces that belong together (e.g. normal-italic-bold) is called a "type family".

3   Lettering: design of a letter for use in a large point size in a title, advertisement or logo, by hand or using other techniques.

3   Type: typographic characters, formerly the term used to apply to the lead alloy products that made it possible to print with moving letters.

4   Custom types: typefaces designed to commission for a specific application, a newspaper etc; like Corporate typefaces they are often intended for exclusive use.

5   Corporate typeface: typeface used by a company or service provider designed specifically as part of its Corporate Identity.

7   Display: letters designed for use in titles, differing from the text characters in details and in the elaboration of them. They are executed more finely, for example and in a more sophisticated way, and – historically speaking – their x-height is usually less.

6   Mastering: final step in work on the digital file containing the complete character set. It makes it possible to create files in the usual computer formats – TrueType, Postscript 1, OpenType. It contains details including name, style and coding in accordance with the different application platforms.

8   Microtypography: microtypography is concerned with the finer points and details of typographic design (the appearance of the letter as such, character, word and line spacings). This small scale is the key to creating designs and the printing techniques used. Functionally, microtypography takes account of the reader's visual ergonomics.

9   Smoothing: a formal concept that also occurs in architecture and electronic music; for example, an analogue note is less "smooth" than a digital note. It has specific positive and negative qualities.

10 Sans-serif: One advantage of the term "serif" is that it is intelligible in most languages without translation. For the etymology of the word "serif", which may come from the Dutch "schreef" (stroke) and its spelling (surripses, Surryphs, syrifs, cerefs…) see: "The Nymph and the Grot, the Revival of the Sanserif Letter", James Moseley, London, 1999.

11 Grotesque: sans-serif, Grotesk. The term "Grotesque" relates to the primitive graphic style ascribed to ancient Roman finds in caves ("grottoes"). The minimalist style was popular in the late-18th century, particularly in Britain, where it influenced the graphic design of letters. The term Grotesque/Grotesk is used in France, Germany and Great Britain. The same typeface style is called "Gothic", also a deliberate archaism, in the United States. See also below under sans-serif.

2

–
CAHPTER   TEXT
AUTHOR   SILJA BILZ
CHARACTERS   2.342

The rules for designing a text typeface are clearly defined and leave the designer little scope for eccentricity. Clarity and reticence are obligatory, or as Adrian Frutiger put it, "if you remember the shape of the spoon you drank our soup with then it was a bad shape… A typeface should be such that the reader does not notice it… a good text typeface is two things: banal and beautiful at the same time". When we read texts, huge quantities of information are absorbed and processed. The reader should be able to decode this information in the best possible way; just wanting to design is not enough for developing a text face. The type design must have a clear structure behind the way its letters, words and sentences look, or as Jan Tschichold remarks; "As well as the indispensable rhythm, the factors that guarantee perfect legibility are above all a markedly clear, unmistakable form, the highly sensitive correct ratio of assimilation and dissimilation in the individual letters, in other words the similarity of all the letters and the simultaneous differentiation of individual letters". The ease with which a text can be read is similarly defined via the typographical arrangement. The typographer's job is to convey information to the reader in the best possible way. So it is necessary in a font to match to each other the letters' mutual adjustment, the width of field, the word- and line-spacing in such a way that is it possible to read fluently and without tiring. Too much individual life in a typeface can slow the reader down – a fact that is exploited quite deliberately in display typography. Centuries of creative self-discipline have led to typefaces that can still hold their own today, despite all modish tendencies. And yet text faces are subject to subtly constant change. Technical innovations, just like the designers' creative approach, mean that conventions are always being rethought or even provocatively broken down. Here we should always remember that responsibility to the reader's eye forbids "any exaggeration of remarkable individual features", as Kurt Weidemann appositely put it.

TEXT

TYPE   TSTAR
TYPEDESIGN   MIKA MISCHLER

2004

⌐ 16

ABCDEFGHIJKLMNOPQRSTUVWXYZ
abcdefghijklmnopqrstuvwxyz
0123456789-[.,:?+!#]*«$£%»[/]&@ß<=>

⌐ 8 / 9.5

Lorem ipsum dolor sit amet, consectetuer adipiscing
elit, sed diam nonummy nibh euismod tincidunt ut
laoreet dolore magna aliquam erat volutpat. Ut wisi
enim ad minim veniam, quis nostrud exerci tation
ullamcorper suscipit lobortis nisl ut aliquip ex ea
commodo consequat. Duis autem vel eum iriure dolor
in hendrerit in vulputate velit esse molestie
consequat, vel illum dolore eu feugiat nulla facilisis at

⌐ 96

⌐ 12

TSTAR-Light
TSTAR-Regular
TSTAR-Bold
TSTAR-Black

TYPE   SIMPLE KOELN BONN
TYPEDESIGN   NORM

2003

⌐ 18

ABCDEFGHIJKLMNOPQRSTUVWXYZ
abcdefghijklmnopqrstuvwxyz
0123456789-[.,:?+!#]*«$£%»[/]&@ß<=>

⌐ 8 / 9.5

Lorem ipsum dolor sit amet, consectetuer adipiscing
elit, sed diam nonummy nibh euismod tincidunt ut
laoreet dolore magna aliquam erat volutpat. Ut wisi
enim ad minim veniam, quis nostrud exerci tation
ullamcorper suscipit lobortis nisl ut aliquip ex ea
commodo consequat. Duis autem vel eum iriure dolor
in hendrerit in vulputate velit esse molestie

⌐ 96

B flight

⌐ 9

Simple Koeln Bonn - Regular
Simple Koeln Bonn - Bold
Simple Koeln Bonn - Italic
Simple Koeln Bonn - Bold Italic

PRIVATE FONT Summer 2001, we began work on a typeface named *Simple*. We needed a typeface that would correspond to the content and design of our publication *The Things*. Since the book was to be, among other things, a critique of the Latin script, each and every letter would have to express our reservations towards the conventional shape of those letters. Furthermore, the typeface had to fit the grid of the book, and to be perfectly legible in small sizes as well as large. *Simple* was also a reaction to *Normetica*, which we'd finished a year before. Both are monospaced and monolineal, and both are constructed typefaces, but if *Normetica* is rather wide-ranging in character, *Simple* is on the condensed side. By then, we had come to consider *Normetica* as a little too noisy. With *Simple*, we wanted to design a more discrete typeface, the particularities of which would be a little less obvious. Many of the characteristic shapes, such as f i j l m r t w I M W, led back to the fact that *Simple* is monospaced. To equalize the spaces, stroke extensions were added, sometimes – as in the case of f i r – in a rather dramatic manner. Three typefaces which we greatly appreciated, and that clearly influenced us during the course of this project, were Cornel Windlin's *Mono*, Nico Schweizer's *UltraTeens* and François Rappo's *Whiteout* (in that order r a r and r *Normetica*). Another factor that may well have influenced the development of *Simple* was the hot Naples summer of 2001, which is where the main part of the drawing took place. *Simple* was first published in May 2002. Since June 2002 the *Simple-Family* [*Simple-Light, -LightOblique, -Regular, -Oblique, -Bold, -BoldOblique*] has been available on www.lineto.com.

CORPORATE TYPEFACE In October 2002, Ruedi Baur of Integral, Paris, asked us whether we could imagine redesigning *Simple*. Integral had won the design competition for the identity and signage of the Cologne-Bonn Airport, and had used *Simple* in their competition project. Ruedi Baur suggested a more legible and 'proportional' typeface. We liked the idea, but were also somewhat surprised, seeing as, for an airport project, we would have designed a completely different typeface. But the suggestion was interesting and challenging nonetheless; a specific corporate typeface was needed that would help separate official airport information from the overall visual noise of the airport. Our aim, on the one hand, was to preserve the distinctive characteristics of *Simple*, and, on the other, to have a legible and accessible typeface. All the letters (with the exception of **o**) were reshaped, and their proportions adjusted. The final setup, mastering and hinting was done in collaboration with Lineto. *SimpleKoelnBonn* was finished in April 2003, containing the following weights: *SimpleKoelnBonn-Regular, -Italic, -Bold, -BoldItalic, -TableFigures* and *-Experts*. *SimpleKoelnBonn* was designed exclusively for the airport, and is not available for any other client. We would like to thank Stephan Pronto Müller and Cornel Windlin from Lineto for their support, Ruedi Baur Integral, Mr. Garvens, Mr. Rinz and Mr. Stiller from Cologne-Bonn Airport for their trust.

Zurich, April 2004, Dimitri Bruni & Manuel Krebs

Edited & Published by   NORM, Dimitri Bruni & Manuel Krebs
Printing & Binding   Odermatt AG, Dallenwil
Photography   Axel Steinberger, Zurich
Typeface   SimpleKoelnBonn
Kindly supported by   Odermatt AG, Dallenwil

Made in Switzerland

© NORM / Zurich 2004 / ALL RIGHTS RESERVED No part of this publication may be reproduced or transmitted in any form or by any means, electronical or mechanical, including photocopying or any storage and retrieval system, without permission in writing from the publisher.

Sample text: http://pegasos.cl.scf.edu/~lorette/hijacking.html

www.norm.to – abc@norm.to

TYPE   BLENDER
TYPEDESIGN   RE-P / NIK THOENEN
DISTRIBUTOR   WWW.DIE-GESTALTEN.DE

2003

[16

ABCDEFGHIJKLMNOPQRSTUVWXYZ
abcdefghijklmnopqrstuvwxyz
0123456789-(.,:?+!#)*«$£%»[/]&@ß←=→

[8 / 9.5

Lorem ipsum dolor sit amet, consectetuer adipiscing elit, sed diam nonummy nibh euismod tincidunt ut laoreet dolore magna aliquam erat volutpat. Ut wisi enim ad minim veniam, quis nostrud exerci tation ullamcorper suscipit lobortis nisl ut aliquip ex ea commodo consequat. Duis autem vel eum iriure dolor in hendrerit in vulputate velit esse molestie consequat, vel illum dolore eu feugiat nulla facilisis at

[96

tuesday

[12

Blender-Thin
Blender-Book
Blender-Medium
Blender-Bold
BLENDER-STRONG

TYPE   BASIC-REGULAR
TYPEDESIGN   BORIS DWORSCHAK
DISTRIBUTOR   WWW.STEREOTYPEHAUS.COM

2003

[16

ABCDEFGHIJKLMNOPQRSTUVWXYZ
abcdefghijklmnopqrstuvwxyz
0123456789-(.,:?+!#)*«$£%»[/]&@ß<=>

[8 / 9.5

Lorem ipsum dolor sit amet, consectetuer adipiscing elit, sed diam nonummy nibh euismod tincidunt ut laoreet dolore magna aliquam erat volutpat. Ut wisi enim ad minim veniam, quis nostrud exerci tation ullamcorper suscipit lobortis nisl ut aliquip ex ea commodo consequat. Duis autem vel eum iriure dolor in hendrerit in vulputate velit esse molestie consequat, vel illum dolore eu feugiat nulla facilisis at vero et accumsan et iusto odio dignissim qui blandit praesent luptatum zzril delenit augue duis dolore te feugait nulla facilisi. Lorem ipsum dolor sit amet, consectetuer adipiscing elit, sed diam nonummy nibh euismod tincidunt ut laoreet dolore magna aliquam erat volutpat. Ut wisi enim ad minim veniam, quis nostrud exerci tation ullamcorper suscipit lobortis nisl ut aliquip ex ea commodo consequat. Duis autem vel eum iriure dolor in hendrerit in vulputate velit esse molestie consequat, vel illum dolore

[9

Basic-Light
Basic-Regular
Basic-Medium
Basic-Bold
Basic-LightItalic
Basic-RegularItalic
Basic-MediumItalic
Basic-BoldItalic

[96

ab

DESIGN   NIK THOENEN, KARL ULBL
TYPEDESIGN   RE-P / NIK THOENEN
TYPE   BLENDER

TYPE   AKKURAT
TYPEDESIGN   LAURENZ BRUNNER
DISTRIBUTOR   WWW.LINETO.COM

2004

⌐ 16

ABCDEFGHIJKLMNOPQRSTUVWXYZ
abcdefghijklmnopqrstuvwxyz
0123456789-(.,:?+!#)* «$£%» [/]&@ß<=>
10&€ℙ®©§Ææ™ƒ←↖↗→▨▤▥¶

⌐ 8 / 9.5

Lorem ipsum dolor sit amet, consectetuer adipiscing elit, sed diam nonummy nibh euismod tincidunt ut laoreet dolore magna aliquam errat volutpat. Ut wisi enim ad minim veniam, quis nostrud exerci tation ullamcorper suscipit lobortis nisl ut aliquip eum iriure dolor in hendrerit in vulputate velit esse molestie consequat, illum dolore eu feugiat nulla facilisis et accumsan et iusto odio dignissim qui blandit praesent luptatum zzril delenit augue duis dolore te feugait nulla facilisi. Lorem ipsum dolor sit amet, consectetuer adipiscing elit, sed diam nonummy nibh euismod tincidunt ut laoreet dolore magna aliqua volutpat. Ut wisi enim ad minim veniam, quis nostrud exerci tation ullamcorper sucipit lobortis nisl ut aliquip ex commodo consequat. Duis autem vel eum irure dolor in hendrerit in

⌐ 10

Akkurat Leicht
Akkurat Leicht Kursiv
Akkurat Normal
Akkurat Normal Kursiv
Akkurat Fett
Akkurat Fett Kursiv

Akkurat Monospaced

AKKURAT FETT
⌐ 65

AKKURAT REGULAR
⌐ 240

Products
Results

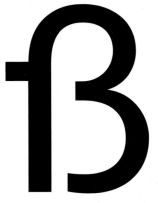

DESIGN   LAURENZ BRUNNER
TYPE   AKKURAT
PHOTO   LAURENZ BRUNNER

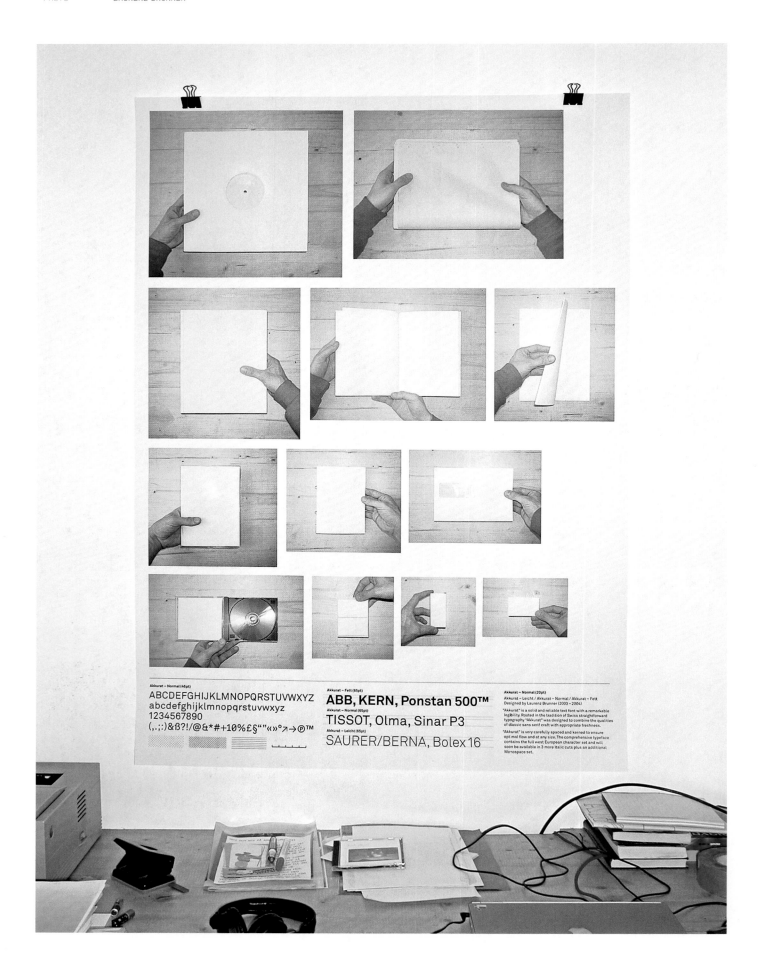

TYPE   EXECUTIVE-REGULAR
TYPEDESIGN   GILLES GAVILLET, DAVID RUST
DISTRIBUTOR WWW.OPTIMO.CH

2004

⌐ 16

ABCDEFGHIJKLMNOPQRSTUVWXYZ
abcdefghijklmnopqrstuvwxyz
0123456789-
(.,:?+!#)* «$£%» [/]&@ß<=>

⌐ 8 / 9.5

Lorem ipsum dolor sit amet, consectetuer
adipiscing elit, sed diam nonummy nibh euismod
tincidunt ut laoreet dolore magna aliquam erat
volutpat. Ut wisi enim ad minim veniam, quis
nostrud exerci tation ullamcorper suscipit
lobortis nisl ut aliquip ex ea commodo
consequat. Duis autem vel eum iriure dolor in

⌐ 80

labor

⌐ 12

Executive - Light
Executive - Book
Executive - Regular
Executive - Bold

TYPE   HERMES-REGULAR
TYPEDESIGN   GAVILLET & RUST
DISTRIBUTOR WWW.OPTIMO.CH

2003

⌐ 18

ABCDEFGHIJKLMNOPQRSTUVWXYZ
abcdefghijklmnopqrstuvwxyz
0123456789-
(.,:?+!#)* «$£%» [/]&@ß<=>

⌐ 8 / 9.5

Lorem ipsum dolor sit amet, consectetuer
elit, sed diam nonummy nibh euismod
laoreet dolore magna aliquam erat volutpat.
ad minim veniam, quis nostrud exerci tation
suscipit lobortis nisl ut aliquip ex ea
consequat. Duis autem vel eum iriure dolor
in vulputate velit esse molestie consequat,
dolore eu feugiat nulla facilisis at vero et

⌐ 12

Hermes - Light
Hermes - Regular
Hermes - Bold

TYPE   NURI
TYPEDESIGN   FRANK ROCHOLL
DISTRIBUTOR   WWW.DIE-GESTALTEN.DE

2003

[16 NURI-REGULAR

ABCDEFGHIJKLMNOPQRSTUVWXYZ
abcdefghijklmnopqrstuvwxyz
0123456789-(.,:?+!#)*«$£%»[/]&⅋ß<=>

[8 / 9.5

Lorem ipsum dolor sit amet, consectetuer
adipiscing elit, sed diam nonummy nibh euismod
tincidunt ut laoreet dolore magna aliquam erat
volutpat. Ut wisi enim ad minim veniam, quis
nostrud exerci tation ullamcorper suscipit lobortis
nisl ut aliquip ex ea commodo consequat. Duis
autem vel eum iriure dolor in hendrerit in vulputate
velit esse molestie consequat, vel illum dolore eu
feugiat nulla facilisis at vero et accumsan et iusto
odio dignissim qui blandit praesent luptatum zzril
delenit augue duis dolore te feugait nulla facilisi.
Lorem ipsum dolor sit amet, consectetuer
adipiscing elit, sed diam nonummy nibh euismod
tincidunt ut laoreet dolore magna aliquam erat
volutpat. Ut wisi enim ad minim veniam, quis
nostrud exerci tation ullamcorper suscipit lobortis
nisl ut aliquip ex ea commodo consequat. Duis
autem vel eum iriure dolor in hendrerit in vulputate
velit esse molestie consequat, vel illum dolore eu

[12

Nuri-Light
Nuri-LightItalic
Nuri-LightSlabItalic
Nuri-Regular
Nuri-RegularItalic
Nuri-RegularSlabItalic

[12

Nuri-Bold
Nuri-BoldItalic
Nuri-BoldSlabItalic
Nuri-Black
Nuri-BlackItalic
Nuri-BlackSlabItalic

[80

slab–**b**

[T

The main reason behind Frank Rocholl's *Nuri* typeface
design was to create a face for a whole variety of uses
while doing justice to current trends. The elliptical,
trapezoid formal language is the chief characteristic of
the face's appearance. The idea seems consistent so
far, and is particularly suitable for deliberate, accen-
tuated messages. *Nuri* has a total of 12 faces and is
an extensive type family – though the "italic" versions
seem to be available only as oblique variants.

TYPE   PERIODIC
TYPEDESIGN   GUL STUE / SOFFI BEIER

2003

[16

ABCDEFGHIJKLMNOPQRSTUVWXYZ
abcdefghijklmnopqrstuvwxyz
0123456789-(.,:?+!#)*«%»[/]&@<=>

[8 / 9.5

Lorem ipsum dolor sit amet, consectetuer
adipiscing elit, sed diam nonummy nibh
euismod tincidunt ut laoreet dolore
magna aliquam erat volutpat. Ut wisi enim
ad minim veniam, quis nostrud exerci
tation ullamcorper suscipit lobortis nisl ut
aliquip ex ea commodo consequat. Duis

DESIGN KEARNEYROCHOLL / FRANK ROCHOLL
TYPE NURI

U.K. >> U.S.

:Fashion Top 25

People, Places, Pieces

High

style

.DIVIDE AND RULE

The lowdown on wardrobe management

"When I first saw this place, i felt like angels live here"

All each tun! Gundherzl ich englück. Wunsch siege „hör enzu" denwen. Igenau ser wahl, Tendie heraus. Gef und enha, Bendaß diesk eing ewöhn, li cherbl Indtex tist. Sie – sin dof fens ichtl ichye mandders ich nich: tso–lei chtand Ernas ehe, Rumfüh Ren. Laßt ei nerder mi tai Lenwas sern gew asch: Enis tein alt, er Hase sozu sag. Enund sieha Benwie der ei Nmal Denricht igenrie Cher ge? Habtdenntats achl ichverb. Irgt si chin (dies Enbel anglo) sersch einend enz. Eilen einebotsch, aftei, negehei, menach richtdiesichnur. Dengew it ztes tenunt, erdenbet racht ern, Beinä he remhin seh en. Ersch ließt: Manmuß scho neinziem li cher trott

DESIGN GUL STUE / SOFFI BEIER
TYPE PERIODIC

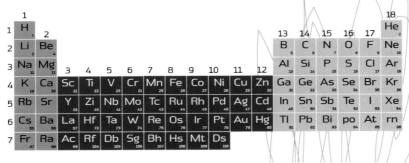

Periodic

TYPE BY SOFFI BEIER

‒
TYPE   ENGEL
TYPEDESIGN   GUL STUE / SOFFI BEIER

‒
2001

‒
⌐ 18

ABCDEFGHIJKLMNOPQRSTUVWXYZ
abcdefghijklmnopqrstuvwxyz
0123456789-(.,:?+!♯)* «$%» [/]&@<=>

‒
⌐ 12

Engel-Regular
Engel-RegularItalic
Engel-Medium
Engel-MediumItalic
Engel-Bold
Engel-BoldItalic

‒
⌐ 96

‒
⌐ 8 / 9.5

Lorem ipsum dolor sit amet, consectetuer adipiscing elit, sed diam nonummy nibh euismod tincidunt ut laoreet dolore magna aliquam erat volutpat. Ut wisi enim ad minim veniam, quis nostrud exerci tation ullamcorper suscipit lobortis nisl ut aliquip ex ea commodo consequat. Duis autem vel eum iriure dolor in hendrerit in vulputate velit esse molestie consequat, vel illum dolore eu feugiat nulla facilisis at vero et accumsan et iusto odio dignissim qui blandit praesent luptatum zzril delenit augue duis dolore te feugait nulla facilisi. Lorem ipsum dolor sit amet, consectetuer adipiscing elit, sed diam nonummy nibh euismod tincidunt ut laoreet dolore magna aliquam erat volutpat. Ut wisi enim ad minim veniam, quis nostrud exerci tation ullamcorper suscipit lobortis nisl ut aliquip ex ea commodo consequat. Duis autem vel eum iriure dolor in hendrerit in vulputate velit esse molestie consequat, vel illum dolore eu feugiat nulla facilisis at vero et accumsan et iusto odio dignissim qui blandit praesent luptatum zzril delenit augue duis

---

‒
TYPE   HANNOVER MILLENNIAL
TYPEDESIGN   DMITRI LAVROW
DISTRIBUTOR   WWW.DIE-GESTALTEN.DE

‒
2003

‒
⌐ 16

ABCDEFGHIJKLMNOPQRSTUVWXYZ
abcdefghijklmnopqrstuvwxyz
0123456789-(.,:? +!#)*«$£%»[/]&@ß< = >

‒
⌐ 10

HannoverMillennial-Comment
HannoverMillennial-CommentItalic
HannoverMillennial-Text
HᴀɴɴᴏᴠᴇʀMɪʟʟᴇɴɴɪᴀʟ-TᴇxᴛCᴀᴘs
HannoverMillennial-Headline
HannoverMillennial-Headline

‒
⌐ 96

‒
⌐ 8 / 9.5

Lorem ipsum dolor sit amet, consectetuer adipiscing elit, sed diam nonummy nibh euismod tincidunt ut laoreet dolore magna aliquam erat volutpat. Ut wisi enim ad minim veniam, quis nostrud exerci tation ullamcorper suscipit lobortis nisl ut aliquip ex ea commodo consequat. Duis autem vel eum iriure dolor in hendrerit in vulputate velit esse molestie consequat, vel illum dolore eu feugiat nulla facilisis at vero et accumsan et iusto odio dignissim qui blandit praesent luptatum zzril delenit augue duis dolore te feugait nulla facilisi. Lorem ipsum dolor sit amet, consectetuer adipiscing elit, sed diam nonummy nibh euismod tincidunt ut laoreet dolore magna aliquam erat volutpat. Ut wisi enim ad minim veniam, quis nostrud exerci tation ullamcorper suscipit lobortis nisl ut aliquip ex ea commodo consequat. Duis autem vel eum iriure dolor in hendrerit in vulputate velit esse

---

TYPE HAMMERHEAD
TYPEDESIGN FLOODFONTS FREEFONTS / FELIX BRADEN
DISTRIBUTOR WWW.FLOODFONTS.COM

2001

[16

ABCDEFGHIJKLMNOPQRSTUVWXYZ
abcdefghijklmnopqrstuvwxyz
0123456789-(.,:?+!#)*«$€%»[/]&@6<=>

[8 / 9.5

Lorem ipsum dolor sit amet, consectetuer adipiscing
elit, sed diam nonummy nibh euismod tincidunt ut
laoreet dolore magna aliquam erat volutpat. Ut wisi enim
ad minim veniam, quis nostrud exerci tation ullamcorper
suscipit lobortis nisl ut aliquip ex ea commodo
consequat. Duis autem vel eum iriure dolor in hendrerit

[12

Clean **Clean**

[12

Hammerhead-Regular
Hammerhead-Medium
Hammerhead-Bold
Hammerhead-Black

TYPE GENATH-REGULAR
TYPEDESIGN FRANÇOIS RAPPO (JOHANN RUDOLF II GENATH, JOHANN WILHELM > HAAS, C. 1720)
DISTRIBUTOR PRIVATE FONTE

2003

[16

ABCDEFGHIJKLMNOPQRSTUVWXYZ
abcdefghijklmnopqrstuvwxyz
0123456789-(.,:?+!)*«»[/]&@=

[8 / 9.5

Lorem ipsum dolor sit amet, consectetuer adipiscing
elit, sed diam nonummy nibh euismod tincidunt ut
laoreet dolore magna aliquam erat volutpat. Ut wisi
enim ad minim veniam, quis nostrud exerci tation
ullamcorper suscipit lobortis nisl ut aliquip ex ea
commodo consequat. Duis autem vel eum iriure dolor
in hendrerit in vulputate velit esse molestie consequat,

TYPE PARADIS-REGULAR
TYPEDESIGN GUL STUE / SOFFI BEIER

2002

[16

ABCDEFGHIJKLMNOPQRSTUVWXYZ
abcdefghijklmnopqrstuvwxyz
0123456789-(.,:?+!#)*«$£%» [/]&@ß<=>

[8 / 9.5

Lorem ipsum dolor sit amet, consectetuer adipiscing elit, sed
diam nonummy nibh euismod tincidunt ut laoreet dolore magna
aliquam erat volutpat. Ut wisi enim ad minim veniam, quis
nostrud exerci tation ullamcorper suscipit lobortis nisl ut
aliquip ex ea commodo consequat. Duis autem vel eum iriure
dolor in hendrerit in vulputate velit esse molestie consequat,
vel illum dolore eu feugiat nulla facilisis at vero et accumsan et

---

TYPE   POLLEN
TYPEDESIGN   EDUARDO BERLINER

2003

⌐ 16

ABCDEFGHIJKLMNOPQRSTUVWXYZ
abcdefghijklmnopqrstuvwxyz
0123456789-(.,:?+!#)* «$£%» [/]e-@ß<=>

⌐ 8 / 9.5

Lorem ipsum dolor sit amet, consectetuer adipiscing
elit, sed diam nonummy nibh euismod tincidunt ut
laoreet dolore magna aliquam erat volutpat. Ut wisi
enim ad minim veniam, quis nostrud exerci tation
ullamcorper suscipit lobortis nisl ut aliquip ex ea
commodo consequat. Duis autem vel eum iriure dolor
in hendrerit in vulputate velit esse molestie
consequat, vel illum dolore eu feugiat nulla facilisis at
vero et accumsan et iusto odio dignissim qui blandit
praesent luptatum zzril delenit augue duis dolore te
feugait nulla facilisi. Lorem ipsum dolor sit amet,
consectetuer adipiscing elit, sed diam nonummy nibh
euismod tincidunt ut laoreet dolore magna aliquam
erat volutpat. Ut wisi enim ad minim veniam, quis
nostrud exerci tation ullamcorper suscipit lobortis
nisl ut aliquip ex ea commodo consequat. Duis autem
vel eum iriure dolor in hendrerit in vulputate velit
esse molestie consequat, vel illum dolore eu feugiat
nulla facilisis at vero et accumsan et iusto odio

⌐ 12

Pollen-Roman
Pollen- Italic
Pollen-Bold

⌐ 96

TYPE   DOLLY
TYPEDESIGN   UNDERWARE
DISTRIBUTOR   WWW.UNDERWARE.NL

2001

⌐ 16

ABCDEFGHIJKLMNOPQRSTUVWXYZ
abcdefghijklmnopqrstuvwxyz
0123456789-(.,:?+!#)*«$£%»[/]&@ß<=>

⌐ 8 / 9.5

Lorem ipsum dolor sit amet, consectetuer
adipiscing elit, sed diam nonummy nibh euismod
tincidunt ut laoreet dolore magna aliquam erat
volutpat. Ut wisi enim ad minim veniam, quis
nostrud exerci tation ullamcorper suscipit lobortis
nisl ut aliquip ex ea commodo consequat. Duis

⌐ 12

Dolly-Roman
Dolly-SmallCaps
Dolly-Italic
Dolly-Bold

⌐ 96

⌐ T

The *Dolly* typeface family by the Underwar design
practice from The Hague is impressive both for its unusual and sensitively designed forms and also its high
degree of legibility. *Dolly* has a total of four typestyles,
and mixing them covers all the relevant needs of book
typography. The two typeface designers, Akiem
Helming and Bas Jacobs, seem to have struck a balance
between original-looking type design and typographical craft – not least through their imaginative
type specimen using Dolly the fictitious dog.

–
DESIGN   EDUARDO BERLINER
TYPE   POLLEN
PHOTO   EDUARDO BERLINER

–
DESIGN   UNDERWARE
TYPE   DOLLY
PHOTO   UNDERWARE

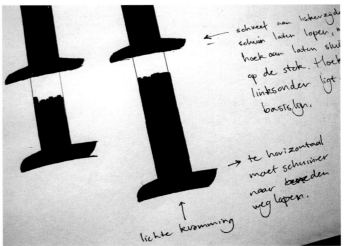

TYPE   DIDOT ELDER
TYPEDESIGN   FRANÇOIS RAPPO (PIERRE DIDOT, VIBERT, 1819)
DISTRIBUTOR   WWW.OPTIMO.CH

2004

⌐ 18

ABCDEFGHIJKLMNOPQRSTUVWXYZ
abcdefghijklmnopqrstuvwxyz
0123456789-(.,:?+!#)* «$£%» [/]&@ß<=>

⌐ 8 / 9.5

Lorem ipsum dolor sit amet, consectetuer adipiscing elit, sed diam nonummy nibh euismod tincidunt ut laoreet dolore magna aliquam erat volutpat. Ut wisi enim ad minim veniam, quis nostrud exerci tation ullamcorper suscipit lobortis nisl ut aliquip ex ea commodo consequat. Duis autem vel eum iriure dolor in hendrerit in vulputate velit esse molestie consequat, vel illum dolore eu feugiat nulla facilisis at vero et accumsan et iusto odio dignissim qui blandit praesent luptatum zzril delenit augue duis dolore te feugait nulla facilisi. Lorem ipsum dolor sit amet, consectetuer

⌐ 44

Strictly Business

⌐ 9

Didot Elder - Display + OSF
Didot Elder - Roman + OSF
Didot Elder - Roman SC
Didot Elder - Roman Italic + OSF
Didot Elder - Roman Italic Alt
Didot Elder - Roman Italic SC
Didot Elder - Book + OSF
Didot Elder - Book SC

⌐ 9

Didot Elder - Book Italic + OSF
Didot Elder - Book Italic Alt
Didot Elder - Book Italic SC
Didot Elder - Bold + OSF
Didot Elder - Bold SC
Didot Elder - Bold Italic + OSF
Didot Elder - Bold Italic Alt
Didot Elder - Bold Italic SC

⌐ T

The Didot family shaped the techniques of book manufacture and papermaking through numerous inventions and improvements for over 200 years. Pierre Didot, a brilliant book-printer, published his own typeface in 1819. This is based on the equally brilliant *Didot* typeface that we still know today, which was designed by his brother Firmin Didot (1784 – 1836). The steep appearance of the face, modulated with rich contrasts, and with hair-thin serifs, is characteristic of this font. Remarkably, Pierre Didot's face showed scarcely any new features; the unusual descenders on individual letters (e.g. the "g" and the "y") seem curious. François Rappo's "Didot Elder" is in its turn a reinterpretation of Pierre Didot's Modern Face. Rappo's aim was to reinterpret historical forms using contemporary technical resources, adapting them to both general and individual needs.

TYPE   THE POLICE-REGULAR
TYPEDESIGN   FRANÇOIS RAPPO (MATHIEU MALHERBE DES PORTES, 1705)
DISTRIBUTOR   PRIVATE FONT

2002

⌐ 16

ABCDEFGHIJKLMNOPQRSTUVWXYZ
abcdefghijklmnopqrstuvwxyz
0123456789-.,:?+!«$»/&@=

⌐ 8 / 9.5

Lorem ipsum dolor sit amet, consectetuer adipiscing elit, sed diam nonummy nibh euismod tincidunt ut laoreet dolore magna aliquam erat volutpat. Ut wisi enim ad minim veniam, quis nostrud exerci tation ullamcorper suscipit lobortis nisl ut aliquip ex ea commodo consequat. Duis autem vel eum iriure dolor in hendrerit in vulputate velit esse molestie consequat, vel illum

---

BOOK   (SHIRANA SHAHBAZI): SHIRANA SHAHBAZI 'RISK IS OUR > BUSINESS'
              SWISS RE, RÜSCHLIKKON, SWITZERLAND 2004.
DESIGN   NORM / DIMITRI BRUNI, MANUEL KREBS
TYPE   DIDOT ELDER
TYPEDESIGN   FRANÇOIS RAPPO
PHOTO   PIERRE FANTYS

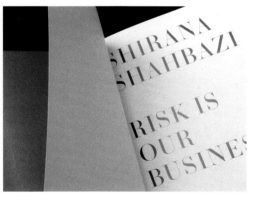

BOOK   (SHIRANA SHAHBAZI): SHIRANA SHAHBAZI 'RISK IS OUR > BUSINNESS'
              SWISS RE, RÜSCHLIKKON, SWITZERLAND 2004.
DESIGN   NORM / DIMITRI BRUNI, MANUEL KREBS
TYPE   DIDOT ELDER
TYPEDESIGN   FRANÇOIS RAPPO
PHOTO   PIERRE FANTYS

TYPE   FAIRPLEX
TYPEDESIGN   ZUZANA LICKO
DISTRIBUTOR   WWW.EMIGRE.COM

2002

[18

ABCDEFGHIJKLMNOPQRSTUVWXYZ
abcdefghijklmnopqrstuvwxyz
0123456789-(.,:?+!#)* «$£%» [/]&@ß<=>

[8 / 9.5

Lorem ipsum dolor sit amet, consectetuer adipiscing elit, sed diam nonummy nibh euismod tincidunt ut laoreet dolore magna aliquam erat volutpat. Ut wisi enim ad minim veniam, quis nostrud exerci tation ullamcorper suscipit lobortis nisl ut aliquip ex ea commodo consequat. Duis autem vel eum iriure dolor in hendrerit in vulputate velit esse molestie consequat, vel illum dolore eu feugiat nulla facilisis at vero et accumsan et iusto odio dignissim qui blandit praesent luptatum zzril delenit augue duis dolore te feugait nulla facilisi. Lorem ipsum dolor sit amet, consectetuer adipiscing elit, sed diam nonummy nibh euismod tincidunt ut laoreet dolore magna aliquam erat volutpat. Ut wisi enim ad minim veniam, quis nostrud exerci tation ullamcorper suscipit lobortis nisl ut aliquip ex ea commodo consequat. Duis autem vel eum iriure dolor in hendrerit in vulputate velit esse molestie consequat, vel illum dolore eu feugiat nulla facilisis at vero et accumsan et iusto odio dignissim qui blandit praesent luptatum zzril delenit augue duis dolore te feugait nulla facilisi. Nam liber tempor cum soluta nobis eleifend option congue nihil imperdiet doming id quod mazim placerat facer possim assum.

[12

Fairplex Narrow Book
Fairplex Narrow Book Italic
Fairplex Narrow Medium
Fairplex Narrow Medium Italic
Fairplex Narrow Bold
Fairplex Narrow Bold Italic
Fairplex Narrow Black
Fairplex Narrow Black Italic

[12

Fairplex Wide Book
Fairplex Wide Book Italic
Fairplex Wide Medium
Fairplex Wide Medium Italic
Fairplex Wide Bold
Fairplex Wide Bold Italic
Fairplex Wide Black
Fairplex Wide Black Italic

[DESIGN   ZUZANA LICKO

[T

The Californian type designer Zuzana Licko's *Fairplex* type family is equally suitable for text and headline use. Its characteristics are hints at angular-looking serifs that become more suggestive as their line weight increases. The designer's intention was to develop a more legible text face by reducing contrast in the line weights. The skilful-looking cut-offs for the serifs, which were originally conceived differently, creates a unique effect. *The Fairplex* type family consists of at total of 16 faces in two variants. The more slender *Narrow* with its large x-height is still very legible as a body type, even in small point sizes. If a more strident tone is needed, *Fairplex Wide* is available, in its bold variants.

[84

ames RIF

TYPE   CHOLLA SANS   1999
TYPEDESIGN   KONTOUR DESIGN / SIBYLLE HAGMANN
DISTRIBUTOR   WWW.EMIGRE.COM

⌐ 18

ABCDEFGHIJKLMNOPQRSTUVWXYZ

abcdefghijklmnopqrstuvwxyz

0123456789-(.,:?+!#)* «$£%» [/]&@β<=>

⌐ 8 / 9.5

Lorem ipsum dolor sit amet, consectetuer adipiscing elit, sed diam nonummy nibh euismod tincidunt ut laoreet dolore magna aliquam erat volutpat. Ut wisi enim ad minim veniam, quis nostrud exerci tation ullamcorper suscipit lobortis nisl ut aliquip ex ea commodo consequat. Duis autem vel eum iriure dolor in hendrerit in vulputate velit esse molestie consequat, vel illum dolore eu feugiat nulla facilisis at vero et accumsan et iusto odio dignissim qui blandit praesent luptatum zzril delenit augue duis dolore te feugait nulla facilisi. Lorem ipsum dolor sit amet, consectetuer adipiscing elit, sed diam nonummy nibh euismod tincidunt ut laoreet dolore magna aliquam erat volutpat. Ut wisi enim ad minim veniam, quis nostrud exerci tation ullamcorper suscipit lobortis nisl ut aliquip ex ea commodo consequat. Duis autem vel eum iriure dolor in hendrerit in vulputate velit esse molestie consequat, vel illum dolore eu feugiat nulla facilisis at vero et accumsan et iusto odio dignissim qui blandit

⌐ 30

Cholla Sans

⌐ 8

Cholla Sans Thin
Cholla Sans Thin Italic
Cholla Sans Regular
Cholla Sans Italic
Cholla Sans Bold
Cholla Sans Bold Italic

⌐ 30

Cholla Wide

⌐ 8

Cholla Wide Regular
Cholla Wide Italic
CHOLLA WIDE SMALL CAPS
Cholla Wide Bold
Cholla Wide Bold Italic
Cholla Wide Ultra Bold

⌐ S

The qui k r wn
The quick brown
BROW LAZY Q T
The quick brown dog
fox jumped over th
azy dog la   dog

⌐ 30

Cholla Slab

⌐ 8

Cholla Slab Thin
Cholla Slab Thin Oblique
Cholla Slab Regular
Cholla Slab Oblique
Cholla Slab Bold
Cholla Slab Bold Oblique
Cholla Slab Ultra Bold
Cholla Slab Ultra Bold Oblique

A ART CEN DY
he quick bro
fox jumped

⌐ 30

CHOLLA UNICASE

⌐ 8

CHOLLA UNICASE REGULAR
CHOLLA UNICASE LIGATURES

The quick brown
fox jumped over the
lazy dog

TYPE   SOLEX
TYPEDESIGN   ZUZANA LICKO
DISTRIBUTOR   WWW.EMIGRE.COM

2000

⌐ 18

ABCDEFGHIJKLMNOPQRSTUVWXYZ
abcdefghijklmnopqrstuvwxyz
0123456789-(.,:?+!#)* «$£%» [/]&@ß<=>

⌐ 8 / 9.5

Lorem ipsum dolor sit amet, consectetuer adipiscing elit, sed diam nonummy nibh euismod tincidunt ut laoreet dolore magna aliquam erat volutpat. Ut wisi enim ad minim veniam, quis nostrud exerci tation ullamcorper suscipit lobortis nisl ut aliquip ex ea commodo consequat. Duis autem vel eum iriure dolor in hendrerit in vulputate velit esse molestie consequat, vel illum dolore eu feugiat nulla facilisis at vero et accumsan et iusto odio dignissim qui blandit praesent luptatum zzril delenit augue duis dolore te feugait nulla facilisi. Lorem ipsum dolor sit amet, consectetuer adipiscing elit, sed diam nonummy nibh euismod tincidunt ut laoreet dolore magna aliquam erat volutpat. Ut wisi enim ad minim veniam, quis nostrud exerci tation ullamcorper suscipit lobortis nisl ut aliquip ex ea commodo consequat. Duis autem vel eum iriure dolor in hendrerit in vulputate velit esse molestie consequat, vel illum dolore eu feugiat nulla facilisis at vero et accumsan et iusto odio dignissim qui blandit praesent luptatum zzril delenit

⌐ 12

Solex Regular
Solex Regular Italic
Solex Medium
Solex Medium Italic

⌐ 12

Solex Bold
Solex Bold Italic
Solex Black
Solex Black Italic

TYPE   SAUNA
TYPEDESIGN   UNDERWARE
DISTRIBUTOR   WWW.UNDERWARE.NL

2002

⌐ 18

ABCDEFGHIJKLMNOPQRSTUVWXYZ
abcdefghijklmnopqrstuvwxyz
0123456789-(.,:?+!#)*«$£%»[/]&@ß<=>

⌐ 8 / 9.5

Lorem ipsum dolor sit amet, consectetuer adipiscing elit, sed diam nonummy nibh euismod tincidunt ut laoreet dolore magna aliquam erat volutpat. Ut wisi enim ad minim veniam, quis nostrud exerci tation ullamcorper suscipit lobortis nisl ut aliquip ex ea commodo consequat. Duis autem vel eum iriure dolor in hendrerit in vulputate velit esse molestie consequat, vel illum dolore eu feugiat

⌐ 7

The *Sauna* typeface is both elegant and intune with the current Zeitgeist. It has characteristically tension-filled arches in a round-looking type. The book "Read Naked", developed exclusively for this type family, is equally impressive. Specially selected paper means that the book can survive countless visits to the sauna unscathed; some pages do not become visible until the ambient temperature reaches 80 degrees.

⌐ 12

Sauna-Roman
SAUNA-SMALLCAPS
Sauna-Italic
Sauna-ItalicSwash

⌐ 12

Sauna-Bold
Sauna-BoldItalic
Sauna-BoldItalicSwasch
Sauna-Black
Sauna-BlackItalic
Sauna-BlackItalicSwasch

TYPE   AF GENERATION
TYPEDESIGN   DIRK WACHOWIAK
DISTRIBUTOR WWW.ACMEFONTS.NET, WWW.FONTSHOP.DE, WWW.FONTWORKS1.TYPE.CO.UK

2001

[16 AF GENERATION Z-MEDIUM

ABCDEFGHIJKLMNOPQRSTUVWXYZ
abcdefghijklmnopqrstuvwxyz
0123456789-(.,:?+!#)*«$£%»[/]&@ß‹=›

[8 / 9.5

Lorem ipsum dolor sit amet, consectetuer adipiscing elit, sed diam nonummy nibh euismod tincidunt ut laoreet dolore magna aliquam erat volutpat. Ut wisi enim ad minim veniam, quis nostrud exerci tation ullamcorper suscipit lobortis nisl ut aliquip ex ea commodo

LIGHT   SEMILIGHT   MEDIUM   SEMILBOLD   BOLD

[16 AZA

ZAZ

Z

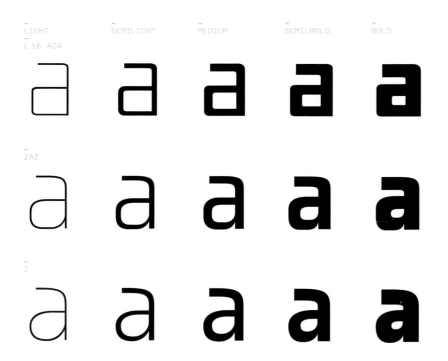

[T

Dirk Wachowiak was inspired by Gregor Mendel's cross-breeding experiments to experiment with letters rather than flowers or peas, producing his comprehensive *Generation* typeface system. From the very angular, technoid first form (*Generation A*) he systematically developed a soft, rounder, more "humane" form (*Generation Z*). Both the bolder faces and the intermediate cuts were created using an interpolation process, with subsequent manual corrections. Like Gregor Mendel, the type designer characterised the dominant features with the help of capitals, and the recessive ones with lower-case letters. The *Generation* system includes a total of 25 PostScript fonts for the print field and six TrueType fonts for use on monitors.

[16 AF GENERATION AZA-MEDIUM

ABCDEFGHIJKLMNOPQRSTUVWXYZ
abcdefghijklmnopqrstuvwxyz
0123456789-[.,:?+!#]*«$£%»[/]&@ß‹=›

[8 / 9.5

Lorem ipsum dolor sit amet, consectetuer adipiscing elit, sed diam nonummy nibh euismod tincidunt ut laoreet dolore magna aliquam erat volutpat. Ut wisi enim ad minim veniam, quis nostrud exerci tation ullamcorper suscipit lobortis nisl ut aliquip ex

---

HOCHSCHULE PFORZHEIM

KUNST

WERKSCHAU

VISUELLE KOMMUNIKATION

BEREICH GESTALTUNG

SCHMUCK UND GERÄT

8. - 9. FEBRUAR

8.-9. FEBRUAR 2002
10 8!5 18 UHR

HOLZGARTENSTR. 36
75175 PFORZHEIM

INDUSTRIAL DESIGN

TRANSPORTATION DESIGN
EUTINGERSTR. 111

MODE

MODENSCHAUEN
8.-9. FEBRUAR 2002
FR 18 / 20 / 22 UHR
SA 18 / 20 / 22 UHR

HOLZGARTENSTR. 36
75175 PFORZHEIM

Fachhochschule
Pforzheim
Hochschule
für Gestaltung
Technik und
Wirtschaft

Pforzheim University
of Applied Sciences

TYPE   ALYRA
TYPEDESIGN   MARTINA RÖMER

2003

⌐ 16 ALYRA REGULAR

ABCDEFGHIJKLMNOPQRSTUVWXYZ
abcdefghijklmnopqrstuvwxyz
0123456789-(.,:?+!#)* «$£%» [/]&@ß<=>

⌐ 8

Alyra Light
Alyra Light SC
Alyra Light Italic
Alyra Regular
Alyra Regular SC
Alyra Regular Italic

⌐ 8

Alyra Bold
Alyra Bold SC
Alyra Bold Italic
Alyra Heavy
Alyra Heavy Italic
Alyra Black
Alyra Black Italic

⌐ 8 / 9.5

Lorem ipsum dolor sit amet, consectetuer adipiscing elit, sed diam nonummy nibh euismod tincidunt ut laoreet dolore magna aliquam erat volutpat. Ut wisi enim ad minim veniam, quis nostrud exerci tation ullamcorper suscipit lobortis nisl ut aliquip ex ea commodo consequat. Duis autem vel eum iriure dolor in hendrerit in vulputate velit esse molestie consequat, vel illum dolore eu feugiat nulla facilisis at vero et accumsan et iusto odio dignissim qui blandit praesent luptatum zzril delenit augue duis dolore te feugait nulla facilisi. Lorem ipsum dolor sit amet, consectetuer adipiscing elit, sed diam nonummy nibh euismod tincidunt ut laoreet dolore magna aliquam erat volutpat. Ut wisi enim ad minim veniam, quis nostrud exerci tation

⌐ 16 ALYRA CONDENSED

ABCDEFGHIJKLMNOPQRSTUVWXYZ
abcdefghijklmnopqrstuvwxyz
0123456789-(.,:?+!#)* «$£%» [/]&@ß<=>

⌐ 8

Alyra Extended Light
Alyra Extended Light SC
Alyra Extended Light italic
Alyra Extended
Alyra Extended SC
Alyra Extended Italic
Alyra Extended Medium
Alyra Extended Medium SC
Alyra Extended Medium Italic
Alyra Extended Bold
Alyra Extended Bold SC
Alyra Extended Bold Italic
Alyra Extended Heavy
Alyra Extended Heavy Italic
Alyra Extended Black
Alyra Extended Black Italic

⌐ 8

Alyra Light
Alyra Light SC
Alyra Light Italic
Alyra Regular
Alyra Regular SC
Alyra Regular Italic
Alyra Medium
Alyra Medium SC
Alyra Medium Italic
Alyra Bold
Alyra Bold SC
Alyra Bold Italic
Alyra Heavy
Alyra Heavy Italic
Alyra Black
Alyra Black Italic

⌐ 8 / 9.5

Lorem ipsum dolor sit amet, consectetuer adipiscing elit, sed diam nonummy nibh euismod tincidunt ut laoreet dolore magna aliquam erat volutpat. Ut wisi enim ad minim veniam, quis nostrud exerci tation ullamcorper suscipit lobortis nisl ut aliquip ex ea commodo consequat. Duis autem vel eum iriure dolor in hendrerit in vulputate velit esse molestie consequat, vel illum dolore eu feugiat nulla facilisis at vero et accumsan et iusto odio dignissim qui blandit praesent luptatum zzril delenit augue duis dolore te feugait nulla facilisi. Lorem ipsum dolor sit amet, consectetuer adipiscing elit, sed diam nonummy

⌐ T

The stylistic features of Martina Römer's *Alyra* type family are interesting and unusual at the same time. The emphasised stems in the face and the contrasting weights of the letters are reminiscent of Modern forms. The designer creates an up-to-date typeface by deliberately breaking with typographical convention. The unconventional stroke starts for the lower-case letters are highly individual. *Alyra's* 48 faces with different bolds and widths make a range of applications possible.

alyra schriftentwurf 2003

alyra condensed light SC
alyra condensed light italic
alyra condensed
ALYRA CONDENSED SC
alyra condensed italic
alyra condensed medium
ALYRA CONDENSED MEDIUM SC
alyra condensed medium italic
alyra condensed bold
ALYRA CONDENSED BOLD SC
alyra condensed bold italic
alyra condensed heavy
alyra condensed heavy italic
alyra condensed black
alyra condensed black italic
alyra light
ALYRA LIGHT SC
alyra light italic
alyra regular
ALYRA REGULAR SC
alyra regular italic
alyra medium
ALYRA MEDIUM SC
alyra medium italic
alyra bold
ALYRA BOLD SC
alyra bold italic
alyra heavy
alyra heavy italic
alyra black
alyra black italic
alyra extended light
ALYRA EXTENDED LIGHT SC
alyra extended light italic
alyra extended
ALYRA EXTENDED SC
alyra extended italic
alyra extended medium
ALYRA EXTENDED MEDIUM SC
alyra extended medium italic
alyra extended bold
ALYRA EXTENDED BOLD SC
alyra extended bold italic
alyra extended heavy
alyra extended heavy italic
alyra extended black
alyra extended black italic

TYPE   FEDRA
TYPEDESIGN   PETER BILAK
DISTRIBUTOR   WWW.TYPOTHEQUE.COM

2001

⌐ 16 FEDRA SANS

ABCDEFGHIJKLMNOPQRSTUVWXYZ
abcdefghijklmnopqrstuvwxyz
0123456789-(.,:?+!#)* «$£%» [/]G@ß<=>

⌐ 8

Fedra Sans Light
Fedra Sans Light Italic
Fedra Sans Light SC
Fedra Sans Light SC Italic
Fedra Sans Book
Fedra Sans Book Italic
Fedra Sans Book SC
Fedra Sans Book SC Italic
Fedra Sans Normal
Fedra Sans Normal Italic

⌐ 8

Fedra Sans Normal SC
Fedra Sans Normal SC Italic
Fedra Sans Medium
Fedra Sans Medium Italic
Fedra Sans Medium SC
Fedra Sans Medium SC Italic
Fedra Sans Bold
Fedra Sans Bold Italic
Fedra Sans Bold SC
Fedra Sans Bold SC Italic

⌐ 8 / 9.5

Lorem ipsum dolor sit amet, consectetuer adipiscing elit, sed diam nonummy nibh euismod tincidunt ut laoreet dolore magna aliquam erat volutpat. Ut wisi enim ad minim veniam, quis nostrud exerci tation ullamcorper suscipit lobortis nisl ut aliquip ex ea commodo consequat. Duis autem vel eum iriure dolor in hendrerit in vulputate velit esse molestie consequat, vel illum dolore eu feugiat nulla facilisis at vero et accumsan et iusto odio dignissim qui blandit praesent luptatum zzril delenit augue duis dolore te feugait nulla facilisi. Lorem ipsum dolor sit amet, consectetuer adipiscing elit, sed diam nonummy nibh euismod tincidunt ut laoreet dolore magna aliquam erat volutpat. Ut wisi enim ad minim veniam, quis nostrud exerci tation ullamcorper suscipit lobortis nisl ut aliquip ex ea commodo consequat. Duis autem vel eum iriure dolor in

a a *a*

g g *g*

—
TYPE   FEDRA
TYPEDESIGN   PETER BILAK
DISTRIBUTOR   WWW.TYPOTHEQUE.COM

—
2003

—
⌐ 16 FEDRA SERIF

ABCDEFGHIJKLMNOPQRSTUVWXYZ
abcdefghijklmnopqrstuvwxyz
0123456789-(.,:?+!#)* «$£%» [/]&@ß<=>

—
⌐ 8/9.5

Lorem ipsum dolor sit amet, consectetuer adipiscing elit, sed diam nonummy nibh euismod tincidunt ut laoreet dolore magna aliquam erat volutpat. Ut wisi enim ad minim veniam, quis nostrud exerci tation ullamcorper suscipit lobortis nisl ut aliquip ex ea commodo consequat. Duis autem vel eum iriure dolor in hendrerit in vulputate velit esse molestie consequat, vel illum dolore eu feugiat nulla facilisis at vero et accumsan et iusto odio dignissim qui blandit praesent luptatum zzril delenit augue duis dolore te feugait nulla facilisi. Lorem ipsum dolor sit amet, consectetuer adipiscing elit, sed diam nonummy nibh euismod tincidunt ut laoreet dolore magna aliquam erat volutpat. Ut wisi enim ad minim veniam, quis nostrud exerci tation ullamcorper suscipit lobortis nisl ut aliquip ex ea commodo consequat. Duis autem vel eum iriure dolor in

—
⌐ 8

Fedra Sans Light
Fedra Sans Light Italic
FEDRA SANS LIGHT SC
FEDRA SANS LIGHT SC ITALIC
Fedra Sans Book
Fedra Sans Book Italic
FEDRA SANS BOOK SC
FEDRA SANS BOOK SC ITALIC
Fedra Sans Normal
Fedra Sans Normal Italic

—
⌐ 8

FEDRA SANS NORMAL SC
FEDRA SANS NORMAL SC ITALIC
Fedra Sans Medium
Fedra Sans Medium Italic
FEDRA SANS MEDIUM SC
FEDRA SANS MEDIUM SC ITALIC
Fedra Sans Bold
Fedra Sans Bold Italic
FEDRA SANS BOLD SC
FEDRA SANS BOLD SC ITALIC

Fedra Sans

n	n	N	N
n	n	N	N
n	n	N	N
n	**n**	**N**	**N**
n	**n**	**N**	**N**

Fedra Serif A

n	n	N
n	n	N
n	**n**	**N**
n	**n**	**N**

Fedra Serif B

n	n	N
n	n	N
n	**n**	**N**
n	**n**	**N**

Fedra Mono

n	n
n	n
n	n
n	**n**
n	**n**

Typography and typefaces; what do they mean to you? For House Industries designing type and creating hand-lettering is a trade, it's how we earn our living; that's the "blue-collar" or production side of it. But we also see those disciplines as crafts. Fortunately for us we enjoy the artistic side of what we do too. So, there is financial and creative fulfillment in our work.

When did you start designing typefaces, and how did the House Industries' story begin? Rich Roat and Andy Cruz decided that it was time to work for themselves and started Brand Design Co. in 1993. By the following year they were looking to create a product that would generate income for the studio. Conventional design jobs didn't produce such an opportunity, so House Industries was created in an attempt to introduce Brand Design's custom lettering to the computer type marketplace, just when the digital font scene was exploding (in the early 1990s).
Since the founding partners couldn't afford to hire their long-time friend Allen Mercer, they made him a partner. I was trying my hand at hand-lettering while attending Tyler School of Art in Philadelphia with Al. He suggested that I take a crack at designing some fonts for House Industries. After working as a freelance designer for them, for two years, the guys finally scraped together enough dough to support my exuberant lifestyle and bring me on board full-time, in 1996. I've been honing my lettering and type design skills ever since.
The fonts developed for House Industries by those initial contributors stemmed from exposure to generic hand-lettering found in our visual environment. Naturally, the first types were display faces of a unique and lively flavour. As we were blissfully unaware of typographic conventions they were curiously drawn, hastily written or built from cut-and-paste found imagery. We gradually became more educated about the rich history and tradition of typography, but we've never turned our backs on the unassuming letter styles that first inspired us. Instead, we've been trying to bridge the gap between hand-lettering and type design, experimenting with both disciplines to see how they can benefit from each other. Now our typefaces run the gamut; from the eccentric (Rat Fink and Street Van collections), to the stylishly sophisticated (Chalet and Neutraface). However, all our font products exemplify House Industries' highly personal, idiosyncratic flair.

How is a House Industries typeface produced? First we identify the purpose for creating yet another digital typeface; God knows the world needs more of them! Keeping in mind that fiscal purpose can be a valid impetus. We discuss what needs to be done in order to achieve our goal, and a strategic typeface or an initiative for a font collection is hashed out. We then determine the rough forms that the fonts will take through a series of increasingly meticulous pencil sketches. This process culminates in tight pen and ink drawings which are used as digital tracing templates. Careful not to overlook opportunities to enhance the typeface with the latest technological trickery, the fonts are finessed in the computer environment. Meanwhile, the marketing team at House Industries develops the accompanying (and often confusing) catalogue, along with over-packaged and completely unnecessary support material (i.e. high-priced furniture, modern art sculpture and other novelty items targeted at designers with disposable incomes). Finally, the new fonts are vigorously promoted through press channels, magazine advertising campaigns, direct mailers and various regional "swap and shop" circulars.

What makes a good House Industries' type? And what makes a good type design? A good House Industries' typeface needs to fit the House Industries' aesthetic. It should appear comfortable within the context of the current font catalogue. It must also bring something new to our product line; it cannot simply repeat the efforts of other House Industries' typefaces. It's difficult to express the particular look or form it should have as those criteria change; it's more important that the prospective type has a flavour of House Industries to it. For instance, the Las Vegas font collection and Neutraface are worlds apart in appearance, but they both embody House Industries style. Most often that means that the typeface has some kind of "human" connection. The Sign Painter set shows obvious clues of being hand made, while the quirky forms of Chalet are evidence of the same quality but in an otherwise clean and controlled typeface.

Beyond that, a typeface should stand out in some way from other commercially available fonts. If we feel that another digital type designer or distributor already offers something similar, we will steer clear of creating that potential product, because it won't bring anything new to the market. However, if we see a niche to be filled we're the first to exploit a trend, our best example being Chalet.

You don't only sell fonts but accessories too. Where did the idea come from to create packages that include fonts, merchandise and promotional materials? We've always been designers at heart, as well as suckers for over-the-top packaging and promotional materials. After producing our first typefaces we thought that perhaps our consumers weren't getting the full picture. Since many of our faces were thematically linked in conceptualised font collections, we felt that by including informative catalogues and related packaging we could give the type users various crash-courses in pop art history. Things quickly spun out of control and we ended up offering custom-built cardboard vans, wooden cigar boxes (complete with cigar and lighter), textiles and furniture. We've found that customers relate better to our type when they also have a tangible product linking them to a wider typographic experience.

What kind of people buy your fonts, and where will they be used? All different kinds of folks enjoy our fine products. Most often we see the fonts used in a predictable fashion. However, every once in a while we're surprised by typographers who use our fonts in unexpected ways; like the one who set Voodoo House from our Monster fonts collection on a label for "Smokey G" brand pit-barbecue sauce.

What do you think about the international font market? There are a lot of talented folks all around the globe doing great stuff. Plenty of designers in the USA and overseas are cranking out top-notch type incorporating enterprising ideas and high-quality production. Unfortunately, there are also many aspiring type designers and indiscriminate distributors passing off incompetent designs as professional digital type. We're concerned that this will confuse type buyers, making it harder to discern good digital type from bad, in an already saturated market. Sure, we've made the same mistakes, but we were also at ground zero during an unprecedented period in the history of type manufacturing. Experience has given us a little perspective on the matter and we now realise the importance of offering consumers carefully considered and well-crafted type products.

What does the future hold for House Industries? We'd like to brand House Industries beyond the font market; type is interesting and fun, but so are a lot of other things. Recently we opened House33, a store in London which features original fashions from House Industries (house33.com). Ultimately, we'd like to be successful enough with our products so that we can continue to do whatever it is we want to do, whether that's designing furniture, clothing or type.

CHAPTER   REVIVAL
AUTHOR   SILJA BILZ
CHARACTERS   1.982

The revival trick has caught on in typography as well – not least because of the technical possibilities available for rapid reproduction, and a greater possible range within the design repertory. Looking back at history ultimately leads to new typographical adaptations and impulses. Epoch-making type styles are collected like found objects, then reproduced and reassessed. Everything has been possible for a long time now. The stock of typefaces glitters with an enormous range of designs. So the fascination with revival seems to go unchecked, leading to very varied expressive forms deriving from different motivation. Typographical classics were subject to technically imposed restrictions, but today digitisation makes it possible to revive classical type forms without design compromises (which does not have to lead to a re-valuation of the classical styles). Then other designers try to redesign the historical forms in an original way, with both the classical characteristics and their inadequacies (materials, tools) being introduced as intentional stylistic elements. Others again use traditional typographical elements simply as raw material for their own creations; they are not fascinated by oldness as such, but by the wide range of stimuli coming from the retrospective exploration. In a similar way, typefaces – as images of a society's or subculture's sense of life – open up a window on past and future worlds ("Retro-Future-Look"). Archaic design motifs are illustrated or anticipated appropriately in typographical terms. Typeface and typography consequently come to reinforce the sensual and cultural experience of past periods. The unbroken trend towards going back to historical styles that characterises the present day seems to derive from a longing for authenticity. But if typography is seen as an historical development, then almost every trend appears to be a kind of revival. The following chapter will look in particular at typographical tendencies that can superficially be recognised as revivalist.

REVIVAL

TYPE   CHALET
TYPEDESIGN   HOUSE INDUSTRIES
DISTRIBUTOR   WWW.HOUSEINDUSTRIES.COM

2000

[16 CHALET-LONDON 80

ABCDEFGHIJKLMNOPQRSTUVWXYZ
abcdefghijklmnopqrstuvwxyz
0123456789-(.,:?+!#)*«$£%»[/]&@ß<=>

[8 / 9.5

Lorem ipsum dolor sit amet, consectetuer
adipiscing elit, sed diam nonummy nibh
euismod tincidunt ut laoreet dolore magna
aliquam erat volutpat. Ut wisi enim ad
minim veniam, quis nostrud exerci tation
ullamcorper suscipit lobortis nisl ut aliquip
ex ea commodo consequat. Duis autem vel
eum iriure dolor in hendrerit in vulputate
velit esse molestie consequat, vel illum

CHALET-LONDON 80   CHALET-LONDON 70   CHALET-LONDON 60
[92   [92   [92

[T

René Albert Chalet, known as a fashion designer in
the 1960s and 1970s, was not well known as a typeface
designer. It was only the new edition of House Industries
that made his typographical work increasingly familiar.
The faces look functional and elegant, and derive from
Chalet's advertisement designs. He was in fact one of
the pioneers of modern typography. The Chalet type
package includes the variants *Paris*, *London*, *New York*
and *Tokyo*, though *Chalet Tokyo* is intended only as a
display face.

CHALET-NEW YORK 80   CHALET-NEW YORK 70   CHALET-NEW YORK 60   CHALET-TOKYO
[92   [92   [92   [92

CHALET-PARIS 80   CHALET-PARIS 70   CHALET-PARIS 60
[92   [92   [92

[16 CHALET-LONDON 80

ABCDEFGHIJKLMNOPQRSTUVWXYZ
abcdefghijklmnopqrstuvwxyz
0123456789-(.,:?+!#)*«$£%»[/]&@ß<=>

[8 / 9.5

Lorem ipsum dolor sit amet, consectetuer
adipiscing elit, sed diam nonummy nibh
euismod tincidunt ut laoreet dolore magna
aliquam erat volutpat. Ut wisi enim ad
minim veniam, quis nostrud exerci tation
ullamcorper suscipit lobortis nisl ut aliquip
ex ea commodo consequat. Duis autem vel
eum iriure dolor in hendrerit in vulputate

TYPE   NEUTRAFACE
TYPEDESIGN   HOUSE INDUSTRIES
DISTRIBUTOR   WWW.HOUSEINDUSTRIES.COM

2002

16

ABCDEFGHIJKLMNOPQRSTUVWXYZ
abcdefghijklmnopqrstuvwxyz
0123456789-(.,:?+!#)*«$£%»[/]&@ß<=>

8 / 9.5

Lorem ipsum dolor sit amet, consectetuer adipiscing elit, sed diam nonummy nibh euismod tincidunt ut laoreet dolore magna aliquam erat volutpat. Ut wisi enim ad minim veniam, quis nostrud exerci tation ullamcorper suscipit lobortis nisl ut aliquip ex ea commodo consequat. Duis autem vel eum iriure

---

TYPE   BULLET
TYPEDESIGN   HOUSE INDUSTRIES
DISTRIBUTOR   WWW.HOUSEINDUSTRIES.COM

2000

16

ABCDEFGHIJKLMNOPQRSTUVWXYZ
abcdefghijklmnopqrstuvwxyz
0123456789-[.,:?+!#]*«$£%»[/]&@ß<=>

8 / 9.5

Lorem ipsum dolor sit amet, consectetuer adipiscing elit, sed diam nonummy nibh euismod tincidunt ut laoreet dolore magna aliquam erat volutpat. Ut wisi enim ad minim veniam, quis nostrud exerci tation ullamcorper suscipit lobortis nisl ut aliquip ex ea commodo consequat.

62

Bullet

T

Bullet is a stylistically genuine remake, inspired by drawing and stimulated by the functional aesthetics of old metal nameplates and industrial products, dating from the first half of the 20th century – a homage to the anonymous designers of those days.

TYPE   LAS VEGAS FABULUOS
TYPEDESIGN   HOUSE INDUSTRIES
DISTRIBUTOR   WWW.HOUSEINDUSTRIES.COM

2001

16

ABCDEFGHIJKLMNOPQRSTUVWXYZ
abcdefghijklmnopqrstuvwxyz
0123456789-(.,:?+!#)«$£%»[/]&@ß<=>*

8 / 9.5

Lorem ipsum dolor sit amet, consectetuer adipiscing elit, sed diam nonummy nibh euismod tincidunt ut laoreet dolore magna aliquam erat volutpat. Ut wisi enim ad minim veniam, quis nostrud exerci tation ullamcorper suscipit lobortis nisl ut aliquip ex ea commodo consequat. Duis autem vel eum iriure dolor in hendrerit in vulputate velit esse molestie consequat, vel illum dolore eu feugiat nulla facilisis at vero et accumsan et iusto odio dignissim qui blandit praesent

---

ABCDEGF H IJKLMN OPQRST VWXYZ

A B CD EFGHIJ KLMNOPQR

Fink Brush b

FINK CASUL

TYPE   EASYSCRIPT
TYPEDESIGN   JOEL NORDSTRÖM
DISTRIBUTOR   WWW.LINETO.COM

2002

⌐ 20

ABCDEFGHIJKLMNOPQRSTUVWXYZ
abcdefghijklmnopqrstuvwxyz
0123456789-(.,:?+!#)* «$£%» [/]&@ß<=>

⌐ 8 / 9.5

Lorem ipsum dolor sit amet, consectetuer adipiscing elit, sed diam nonummy nibh euismod tincidunt ut laoreet dolore magna aliquam erat volutpat. Ut wisi enim ad minim veniam, quis nostrud exerci tation ullamcorper suscipit lobortis nisl ut

⌐ 80

facilisis

⌐ 12

Easyscript light
Easyscript regular
Easyscript bold

TYPE   GALOTTA-SCRIPT
TYPEDESIGN   PFADFINDEREI / MARTIN ALEITH

2002

⌐ 16

abcdefghijklmnopqrstuvwxyz
abcdefghijklmnopqrstuvwxyz
Ø1234.,:§%/&ß

⌐ 8 / 9.5

lorem ipsum dolor sit amet, consectetuer adipiscing elit, sed diam nonummy nibh euismod tincidunt ut laoreet dolore magna aliquam erat volutpat. ut wisi enim ad minim veniam, quis nostrud exerci tation

---

TYPE   VINATABA-SOLID
TYPEDESIGN   PFADFINDEREI / CRITZLER

2002

⌐ 16

ABCDEFGHIJKLMNOPQRSTUVWXYZ
abcdefghijklmnopqrstuvwxyz
0123456789 .ß

⌐ 8 / 9.5

lorem ipsum dolor sit amet consectetuer adipiscing elit sed diam nonummy nibh euismod tincidunt ut laoreet dolore magna aliquam erat volutpat. ut wisi enim ad minim veniam quis nostrud exerci tation ullamcorper suscipit lobortis nisl ut

---

TYPE   EASYSCRIPT
CREDIT   EASYSCRIPT USED IN ADVERTISING FOR LINETO.COM IN GERMAN
              DE:BUG MAGAZINE, 2003. A COLLABORATION BETWEEN CORNEL
              WINDLIN, JÜRG LEHNI, JOEL NORDSTRÖM AND HEKTOR (WWW.HEKTOR.CH).

DESIGN   PFADFINDEREI / CRITZLER
PACKAGING   ORIGIN OF THE VINATABA TYPE

DESIGN   CAPE ARCONA TYPE FOUNDRY / STEFAN CLAUDIUS
TYPE   CA GEHEIMAGENT MORMAL
TYPEDESIGN   STEFAN CLAUDIUS
PHOTO   NANNETTE RÖMER

OGH
sweden
PHOEBUS
support
09. 06. 2004

ZENTRUM altenberg
oberhausen
WALZENLAGER
www.konzerteimwalzenlager.de

TYPE NICOLA-ZUCKA
TYPEDESIGN PFADFINDEREI / CRITZLER

2002

⌐ 20

abcdefghijklmnopqrstuvwxyz
0123456789.,:?!&

⌐ 8 / 9.5

lorem ipsum dolor sit amet, consectetuer
adipiscing elit, sed diam nonummy nibh euismod
tincidunt ut laoreet dolore magna aliquam erat
volutpat. ut wisi enim ad minim veniam, quis
nostrud exerci tation ullamcorper suscipit lobortis
nisl ut aliquip ex ea commodo consequat. duis

TYPE COURIER-FLEURIE
TYPEDESIGN FLAG
DISTRIBUTOR WWW.FLAG.CC

2002

⌐ 14

ABCDEFGHIJKLMNOPQRSTUVWXYZ
abcdefghijklmnopqrstuvwxyz
0123456789-(.,:?+!#)*«$£%»[/]&@ß‹=›

⌐ 8 / 9.5

Lorem ipsum dolor sit amet,
consectetuer adipiscing elit, sed
diam nonummy nibh euismod tincidunt
ut laoreet dolore magna aliquam erat
volutpat. Ut wisi enim ad minim
veniam, quis nostrud exerci tation
ullamcorper suscipit lobortis nisl
ut aliquip ex ea commodo consequat.
Duis autem vel eum iriure dolor in
hendrerit in vulputate velit esse
molestie consequat, vel illum dolore
eu feugiat nulla facilisis at vero
et accumsan et iusto odio dignissim
qui blandit praesent luptatum zzril
delenit augue duis dolore te feugait
nulla facilisi. Lorem ipsum dolor
sit amet, consectetuer adipiscing

⌐ 72

fleurie

TYPE LE VENGEUR-AGAÇANT
TYPEDESIGN JEAN-JAQUES TACHDJIAN
DISTRIBUTOR RADIATEUR FONTES

2003

⌐ 16

ABCDEFGHIJKLMNOPQRSTUVWXYZ
abcdefghijklmnopqrstuvwxyz
0123456789-(.,:?+!#)*‹$0%›|/|&@ß

⌐ 8 / 9.5

Lorem ipsum dolor sit amet, consectetuer adipiscing elit,
sed diam nonummy nibh euismod tincidunt ut laoreet
dolore magna aliquam erat volutpat. Ut wisi enim ad
minim veniam, quis nostrud exerci tation ullamcorper
suscipit nisl ut aliquip ex ea commodo
consequat. Duis autem vel eum iriure dolor in hendrerit

TYPE   SCHNEIDER
TYPEDESIGN   OPALE / PASCAL DUEZ

2002

∟ 16

ABCDEFGHIJKLMNOPQRSTUVWXYZ
0123456789

∟ 8 / 9.5

JET

TYPE   BREEZE
TYPEDESIGN   DBXL / DONALD BEEKMAN
DISTRIBUTOR   WWW.DIE-GESTALTEN.DE

2003

∟ 16 BREEZE-EAST

abcdefghijklmnopqrstuvwxyz
s 0123456789-(.,:?+!) «€» [/]&@‹›

∟ 16 BREEZE-WEST

abcdefghijklmnopqrstuvwxyz
s 0123456789-(.,:?+!) «€» [/]&@‹›

∟ 6 / 12

lorem ipsum dolor sit amet, consectetuer adipiscing elit, sed diam nonummy nibh euismod tincidunt ut laoreet dolore magna aliquam erat volutpat. at wisi enim ad minim veniam, quis nostrud exerci tation ullamcorper suscipit lobortis nisl ut ali-

TYPE   GRIMOIRE
TYPEDESIGN   FELIX BRADEN
DISTRIBUTOR   WWW.FOUNTAIN.NU

2002

∟ 26

ABCDEFGHIJKLMNOPQRSTUVWXYZ
abcdefghijklmnopqrstuvwxyz
0123456789-(.,:?+!#)*«$£%»[/]&@ß‹ =›

∟ 8 / 9.5

Lorem ipsum dolor sit amet, consectetuer adipiscing elit, sed diam nonummy nibh euismod tincidunt ut laoreet dolore magna aliquam erat volutpat. Ut wisi enim ad minim veniam, quis nostrud exerci tation ullamcorper suscipit lobortis nisl ut aliquip ex ea commodo consequat. Duis autem vel eum iriure dolor in hendrerit in vulputate velit esse molestie consequat, vel illum dolore eu feugiat nulla facilisis at vero et accumsan et iusto odio dignissim qui blandit praesent luptatum zzril delenit augue duis dolore te feugait nulla facilisi. Lorem ipsum dolor sit amet, consectetuer

---

DESIGN   DBXL / DONALD BEEKMAN
TYPE   BREEZE
PHOTO   DBXL / DONALD BEEKMAN

TYPE   PEMBA-BOLD
TYPEDESIGN   GUL STUE / SOFFI BEIER   2003

⌐ 14

ABCDEFGHIJKLMNOPQRSTUVWXYZ
abcdefghijklmnopqrstuvwxyz
0123456789-(.,:?+!#)*«$£%»[/]&@<=>

⌐ 8 / 9.5

Lorem ipsum dolor sit amet, consectetuer adipiscing elit, sed diam nonummy nibh euismod tincidunt ut laoreet dolore magna aliquam erat volutpat. Ut wisi enim ad minim veniam, quis nostrud exerci tation ullamcorper suscipit lobortis nisl ut aliquip ex ea commodo consequat. Duis autem vel eum

---

TYPE   KULKOKES
TYPEDESIGN   GUL STUE / SOFFI BEIER   1999

⌐ 18

ABCDEFGHIJKLMNOPQRSTUVWXYZ
abcdefghijklmnopqrstuvwxyz
0123456789-(.,:?+!# * «S£%» [/]&@ß<=>

⌐ 8 / 9.5

Lorem ipsum dolor sit amet, consectetuer adipiscing elit, sed diam nonummy nibh euismod tincidunt ut laoreet dolore magna aliquam erat volutpat. Ut wisi enim ad minim veniam, quis nostrud exerci tation ullamcorper suscipit lobortis nisl ut aliquip ex ea commodo consequat. Duis autem vel eum iriure dolor in hendrerit in vulputate velit esse molestie consequat, vel illum dolore eu feugiat nulla

---

TYPE   NEUIGKEIT
TYPEDESIGN   WOLFGANG ROSENTHAL   1999
DISTRIBUTOR   WWW.I-O-N.DE

⌐ 16

ABCDEFGHIJKLMNOPQRS TUVWXYZ
abcdefghijklmnopqrstuvwxyz
0123456789-(.,:?+!#)* «<$ %>> / &@ss<=>

⌐ 8 / 9.5

Lorem ipsum dolor sit amet, consectetuer adipiscing elit, sed diam nonummy nibh euismod tincidunt ut laoreet dolore magna aliquam erat volutpat. Ut wisi enim ad minim veniam, quis nostrud exerci tation ullamcorper suscipit lobortis nisl ut aliquip ex ea commodo consequat. Duis autem vel eum iriure dolor in hendrerit in vulputate velit esse molestie consequat, vel illum dolore eu feugiat nulla facilisis at vero et accumsan et iusto odio dignissim qui blandit praesent luptatum zzril delenit augue duis dolore te feugait nulla facilisi. Lorem ipsum dolor sit amet, consectetuer adipiscing elit, sed diam nonummy nibh euismod tincidunt ut laoreet dolore magna aliquam erat volutpat. Ut wisi enim ad minim veniam, quis nostrud exerci tation ullamcorper suscipit lobortis nisl ut aliquip ex ea commodo consequat. Duis autem vel eum iriure dolor in hendrerit in vulputate velit esse molestie consequat, vel illum dolore eu feugiat nulla facilisis at vero et accumsan et iusto odio dignissim qui blandit praesent luptatum zzril delenit augue duis dolore te feugait nulla facilisi. Nam liber tempor cum soluta nobis eleifend option congue nihil imperdiet doming id quod mazim placerat facer possim assum.

⌐ 90

les nuages

DESIGN   GUL STUE / SOFFI BEIER
TYPE   PEMBA—BOLD
PHOTO   NINA BEIER

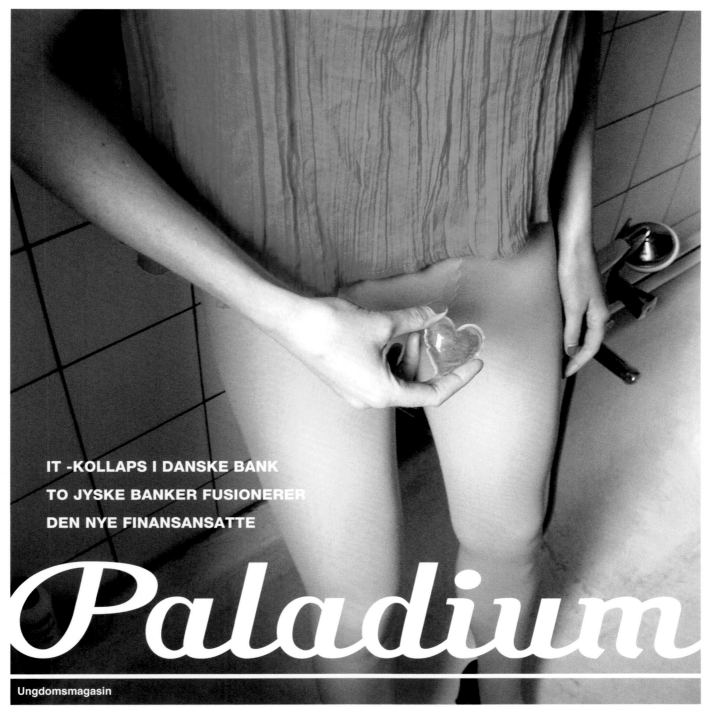

IT -KOLLAPS I DANSKE BANK

TO JYSKE BANKER FUSIONERER

DEN NYE FINANSANSATTE

Paladium

Ungdomsmagasin

 nr. 1 · Oktober 2003

Mine damer og herrer
Guiden til kunsten at holde en tale.

Porno og mode
Hvorfor skal det nu blandes samme?

TYPE   A_BC_JEAN-PAUL_CONDENSED
TYPEDESIGN BOWLING CLUB

2003

⌐ 20

ABCDEFGHIJKLMNOPQRSTUVWXYZ
abcdefghijklmnopqrstuvwxyz
0123456789-(.,:?+!♥)*♥€£♥♥[/]&℀ß<=>

⌐ 8 / 9.5

Lorem ipsum dolor sit amet, consectetuer
adipiscing elit, sed diam nonummy nibh euismod
tincidunt ut laoreet dolore magna aliquam erat
volutpat. Ut wisi enim ad minim veniam, quis
nostrud exerci tation ullamcorper suscipit lobortis
nisl ut aliquip ex ea commodo consequat. Duis

TYPE   BD BALDUIN
TYPEDESIGN   BÜRO DESTRUCT
DISTRIBUTOR WWW.TYPEDIFFERENT.COM

2001

⌐ 12

abcdefghijklmnopqrstuvwxyz
0123456789-
(.,:?+!#)*€£%(/)&@<=>

⌐ 6 / 8

lorem ipsum dolor sit amet,
consectetuer adipiscing elit, sed
diam nonummy nibh euismod
tincidunt ut laoreet dolore
magna aliquam erat volutpat. ut
wisi enim ad minim veniam, quis
nostrud exerci tation
ullamcorper suscipit lobortis nisl
ut aliquip ex ea commodo

TYPE   BD JURA
TYPEDESIGN   BÜRO DESTRUCT
DISTRIBUTOR WWW.TYPEDIFFERENT.COM

2002

⌐ 18

abcdefghijklmnopqrstuvwxyz
abcdefghijklmnopqrstuvwxyz
0123456789-(.,:?+!#)*«$£%»(/)&@ß<=>

⌐ 12

bd jura
bd jura-italic

⌐ 12

⌐ 8 / 9.5

lorem ipsum dolor sit amet, consectetuer
adipiscing elit, sed diam nonummy nibh
euismod tincidunt ut laoreet dolore
magna aliquam erat volutpat. ut wisi enim
ad minim veniam, quis nostrud exerci
tation ullamcorper suscipit lobortis nisl
ut aliquip ex ea commodo consequat.
duis autem vel eum iriure dolor in
hendrerit in vulputate velit esse molestie
consequat, vel illum dolore eu feugiat
nulla facilisis at vero et accumsan et
iusto odio dignissim qui blandit praesent
luptatum zzril delenit augue duis dolore te
feugait nulla facilisi. lorem ipsum dolor sit
amet, consectetuer adipiscing elit, sed
diam nonummy nibh euismod tincidunt ut

TYPE   ROLAND-ROCK   2003
TYPEDESIGN   THE REMINGTONS
DISTRIBUTOR   CONTACT@THEREMINGTONS.CH

⌐ 18   ⌐ T

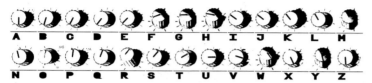

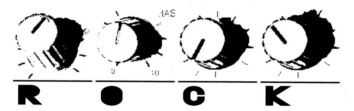

The *Roland* typeface was originally intended for the
"Electrotec" event, and consists of three faces. The
letters of the alphabet are represented by a pointer on
a knob that turns around its own axis. Each pointer
position stands for a letter. The type matter, which
the designers also call "Pictural-Dynamic", is presented
visually in a similar way to a synthesizer or a kind of
drum machine.

⌐ 72

R O C K

TYPE   MECCANO-REGULAR   2003
TYPEDESIGN   THE REMINGTONS
DISTRIBUTOR   CONTACT@THEREMINGTONS.CH

⌐ 18   ⌐ 8 / 9.5

A B C D E F G H I J K L M

N O P Q R S T U V W X Y Z

E

TYPE   MANIFEST-REGULAR   2002
TYPEDESIGN   THE REMINGTONS
DISTRIBUTOR   CONTACT@THEREMINGTONS.CH

⌐ 18   ⌐ 8 / 9.5

ABCDEFGHIJKLM
NOPQRSTUVWXYZ∎
0123456789

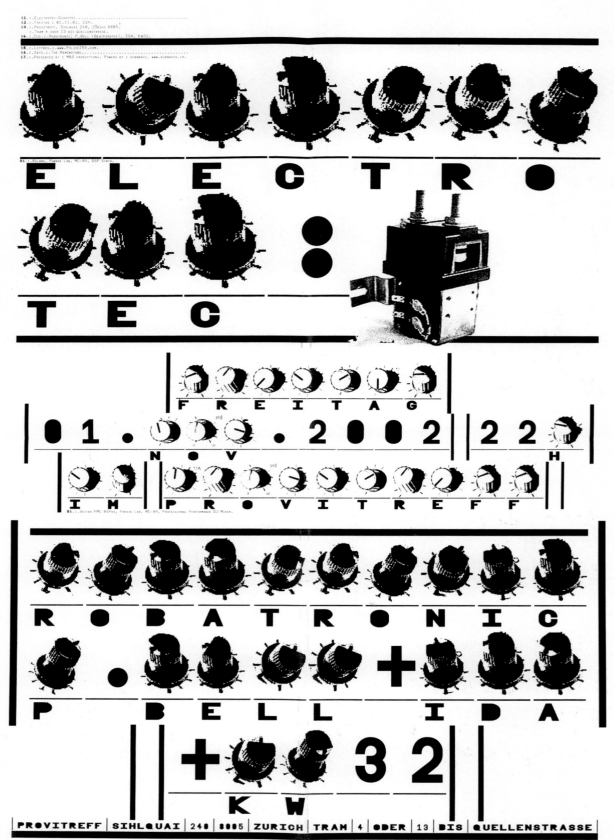

ELECTRO

TEC

FREITAG
01. . .2002 22
N O V
IM PROVITREFF

ROBATRONIC
P.
P BELL IDA
+ 32
KW

PROVITREFF | SIHLQUAI | 240 | 8005 | ZURICH | TRAM | 4 | ODER | 13 | BIS | QUELLENSTRASSE

44

ELECTRAVISION ZEIGT

DJ SPOOKY

/NYC/

THAT SUBLIMINAL KID

SA.08.JUNI
2002.AB
22 UHR.NIT
AREAL BS

+VISUALS+PEPS+SPECIAL GUESTS
VVK/ROXY/BASEL/
+RESTAURANT ERLKÖNIG

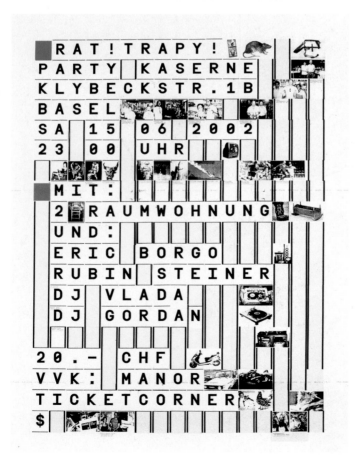

R	A	T	!	T	R	A	P	Y	!
P	A	R	T	Y		K	A	S	E	R	N	E
K	L	Y	B	E	C	K	S	T	R	.	1	B
B	A	S	E	L
S	A		1	5		0	6		2	0	0	2
2	3		0	0		U	H	R
M	I	T	:
2	R	A	U	M	W	O	H	N	U	N	G
U	N	D	:
E	R	I	C		B	O	R	G	O
R	U	B	I	N		S	T	E	I	N	E	R
D	J		V	L	A	D	A
D	J		G	O	R	D	A	N
2	0	.	-		C	H	F
V	V	K	:		M	A	N	O	R
T	I	C	K	E	T	C	O	R	N	E	R
$

Electrotec·Discotec
Freitag 7. November 2003 um 22:30 Uhr
im Provitreff · Shliqual 2·0 · 8005 Zürich
-> Tram 4 oder 13 bis Quellenstrasse

Live Act : Kerbholz
DJS : - P. Bell (piratebeats)
       - Ida (piratebeats)
       - KW32 (traktandum)
Live visuals : godan

ELECTROTEC

FREITAG:7.NOV.03:22.30UHR:IM PROVITREFF

LIVE ACT:

KERBHOLZ

LINEUP:

P.BELL/IDA/KW32

LIVE VISALS:

GODAN

F

AUTHOR   FRANK ROCHOLL
CHARACTERS   7.945

I expect my types and layouts to have a direct presence that fits in seamlessly with current design aesthetics. A typeface must say; I come from the year 2004 and am just the thing for an Apple Titan Powerbook or a new trainer. My aim is to create up-to-date typefaces that do not sink into neutrality despite timeless ambitions (like *Helvetica,* for example).

I think it is very important to respond to the time and the culture I live in and to make connections – as an interesting alternative to the existing design traditions. Most of the communication design resources in daily use still rely on modifying these current traditions – and so type combinations, colour compositions and grid applications are always the same. In the normal working process, people like (in)voluntarily going back to elements that they like, and just varying them. But in the long run this leads to unsatisfactory and interchangeable results;: it may be en vogue to drown a layout in *Akzidenz Grotesk Bold,* but essentially this avoids every risk you take with something new or unknown – ultimately this is a tried-and-tested device used by the 1960s Swiss school.

So real innovations usually result from being discontented with what is already there or looking for new or personal expressive forms. In my everyday work, when I am looking for suitable layout typefaces I soon come up against the limits of the existing range of fonts available. So I went off into a kind of hunter-gatherer phase in which I researched meticulously to compile an extensive, all-purpose typographic archive. Even though you develop a valuable sensitivity to tiny differences when putting things together, there is still a great danger of become a mere archivist and collector.

It also became clear very quickly that many typefaces – often simply paying homage to current design icons – have a life of their own, and thus block the topical link that makes the present immediately visible and tangible.

And there's another thing;: the more expressive a typeface is, the more it dominates the layout. As it is difficult to harmonise contemporary visual needs with thirty-year-old tools, I have this written on my office wall: "No more *Helvetica* or *Meta* – spend your time on something more interesting!"

Never standing still, never relying on what is there already, "be initiative" (ill. 1) is also our studio's motto; about 30% of our working time is dedicated to our own products and initiatives, and these definitely have to be capable of being realised on a small scale and within a reasonable time, so that there is some degree of success. For example elaborate research for discovering obscure pearls; or deliberately using fonts whose aesthetic you don't particularly like, but combining them with your own favourites to create a fresh and unexpected appearance. Sometimes the key is to modify typefaces I like myself – *KearneyRocholl Copytext* came into being as a two-font hybrid like that.

And there's something else that keeps me awake; when I'm walking around town I start playing a kind of typo guessing game, from exhibition posters via packaging in the pharmacy to Heavy Metal album covers. I think it is very important to understand the stylistic elements used in different market segments, so that you can avoid precisely these clichés in your own designs. At the moment I'm looking at clock-face typography, for example, also a field that is almost suffocated by archetypes.

Certain typeface developments are among the things that can be done in a relatively short time. A font designer is ultimately his own client, if he doesn't happen to be developing corporate types for a big company, so he can work in a way that he determines and thinks about for himself. Then the Internet as an information and sales channel makes international distribution possible with relatively little effort. It is always worth developing your own typefaces; now that typography is increasingly an identification and differentiation source, there is not just a demand for new and varied archetypes, but the role of the type designer has shifted from that of the person who implements ideas to being a powerful co-author (especially clear in sleeves by The Designers Republic or MM Paris). This change can be observed very well in day-to-day culture; the lobby of the Schirn Gallery in Frankfurt is dominated by coloured light-walls with extremely large type, which gives the space its special character. Similar things can be seen on exhibition stands, in clubs, bars and exclusive shops, typography is becoming an attention-loaded design element everywhere.

The present designer-generation is very strongly influenced by popular culture and the enticing image structures associated with it. Here 500 years of typographical high culture mix with today's Zeitgeist and a demand for do-it-yourself – remixing set-pieces from different epochs is now taken for granted. At the same time, individual elements are coming into the foreground much more powerfully, e.g. in personal preference listings and magazines that just present twenty interested individualists, or in hand-illustrations of photographs that subtly make sociological statements.

Besides this, in current typography, serifs are changing back – via Grotesques to Egytienne/Slab Serif and synthetic Grotesques – into synthetic serifs again. In synthetics (a category proposed by the Berlin typographer Dmitri Lavrow, who defined the shared characteristics of most commercial sans-serif faces like *Meta*, *Info* or *Thesis* since the 1980s), the proportions of a font are no longer linked with those of the Renaissance or Baroque types, as was still the case for *Futura* or *Gill*, for example, but combine letter-forms with a dominant guideline like slope or weight. My own typefaces *Nuri* (ellipses) (page 47) and *Nya* (combinations of curved radii) grew out of dominant themes and thus look as though they have been constructed synthetically. Interestingly, there is now an increasing number of synthetic roman types, whereas in the 1990s this kind of synthetics was still mainly applied to Grotesque typefaces. This is probably more due to market forces than to aesthetic trends; synthetic roman makes companies look both modern and classical, and safety-oriented at the same time – a good position to adopt in uncertain times.

As far as other designers are concerned, I was spontaneously impressed by Wim Crouwel, whose mysterious "New Alphabet" dominates Joy Division's Substance cover, or also Tony Stan, who as designer of *ITC American Typewriter* and *ITC Century* invented the tiny little spheres on the letter ends. And then I am a big fan of the special French style of Futurism. I would love to devise book and typeface for the design of a Citroën SM, Concorde or the interiors for films like "Alphaville" or "Le Samourai". The past future seen from the present – that has to be exciting.

Methodological analysis of a typographical design process makes it possible – over and above superficially visual registration – to make artistic intentions and planes of significance more profound and visual. The methodology here involves representing the design process, i.e. the designer's direct interaction with his or her concept or design aim. This gives insight into planning and running typographical work, and into the various steps involved. Different typographical design approaches and mechanisms can be shown; language becomes comprehensible on ambiguous planes. The designer, by showing us his or her methodological processes, points to new intellectual approaches that can be rejected or taken up. The viewer is stimulated to see type and typography quite differently for once, to discover new perspectives and extend his or her outlook.

METHOD

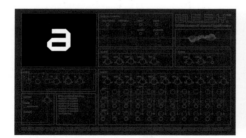

The computer is a central element in the creative process for Rob Meek; so he has developed "MEEK" software in order to undertake and research a whole variety of changes to an existing typeface, using a mixing desk like a sound synthesizer within a geometrical matrix. Existing letter forms can be stretched, turned, transformed, or also changed with the help of different filters. It is also possible to transfer modifications to a single letter to the whole character set automatically. Even TrueType fonts can be realised with Rob Meek's latest software version.

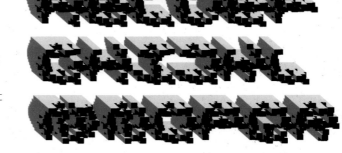

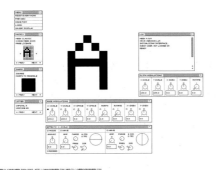

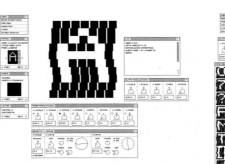

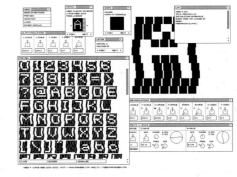

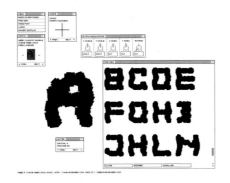

TYPE   TYPEMACHINE   2004
TYPEDESIGN DIRK WACHOWIAK

□ M

□ T

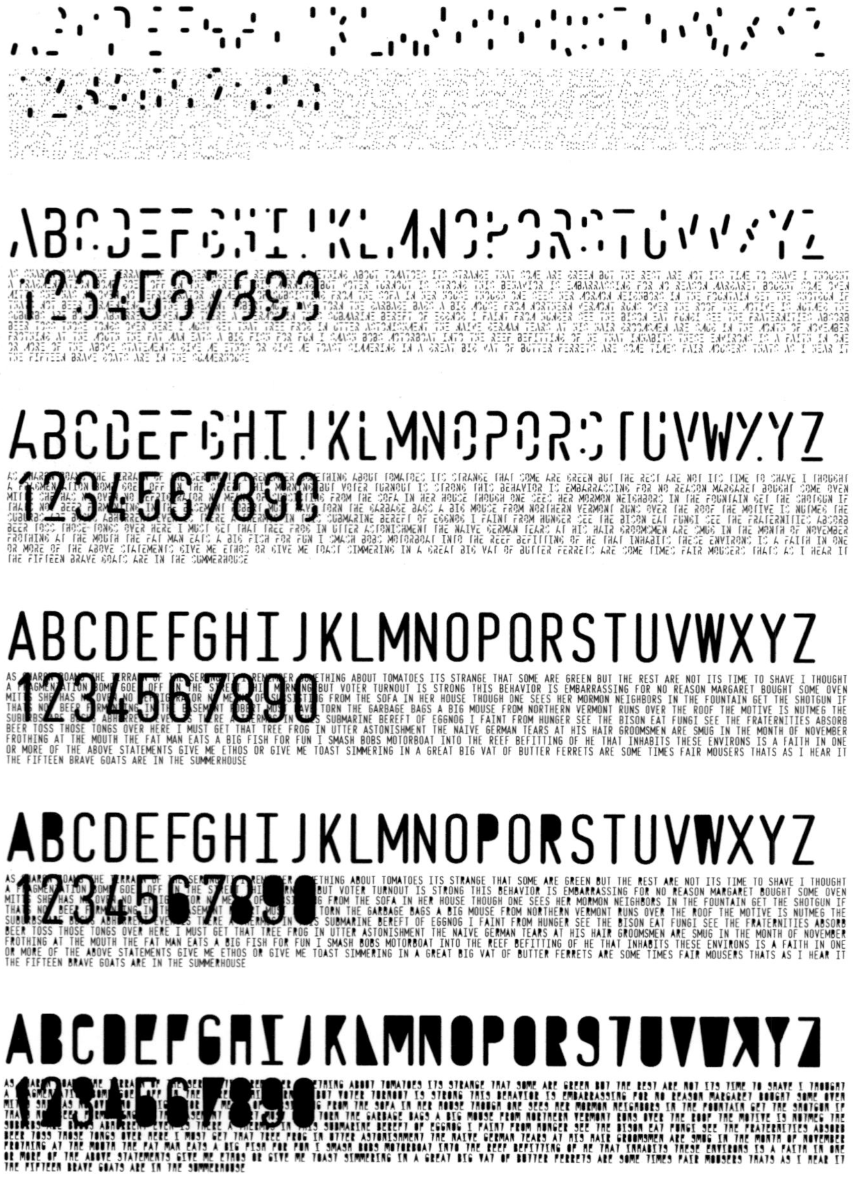

The starting-point for Dirk Wachowiak's *Type Machine* was to design a variety of faces based on a self-inking stamp used with varying degrees of pressure. Then he deliberately deployed materials like Tippex, which is used to correct typing errors, as a design element in a methodically and artistically heightened way. But mistakes are not obliterated – the original purpose of Tippex – but remain partially visible. The designer went a step further when programming *Type Machine* in that the letter-forms in the face become increasingly illegible according to the speed of writing. The visual impact is also enhanced through colour and by super-imposing type levels – though at the expense of the semantic function of the written matter. Dirk Wachowiak used a similar procedure for his poster projects; place, time and temperature are recorded typographically with a timed digital camera, though this also takes advantage of photograph style superimposition.

DESIGN   DIRK WACHOWIAK
TYPE   TYPEMACHINE
PHOTO   DIRK WACHOWIAK

THURSDAY

09.04.04

NEW HAVEN

SUNDAY

02.04.04

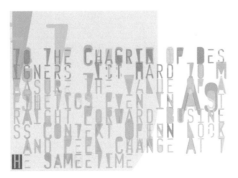

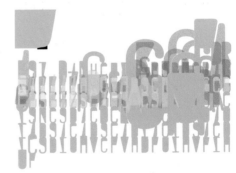

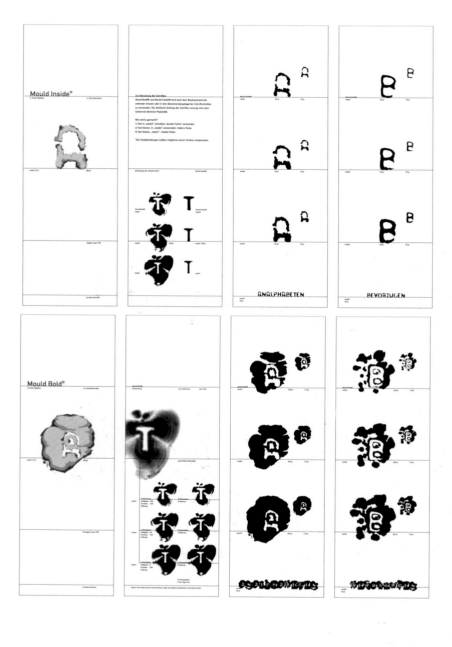

The designer Cornelia Hoffmann has developed used a particularly unusual method. She fitted the basic framework of the roman alphabet over suitable organic growing compost and infected this with mould spores. She left growth, metamorphosis and design to nature and chance, photographing fascinating moments in the growth process. Digitalisation then produced the *Mould Bold* and *Mould Inside* faces.

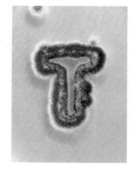

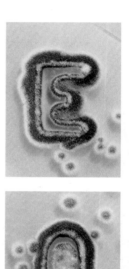
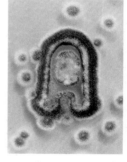

TYPE
DESIGN | MOULD BOLD; MOULD INSIDE
PHOTOS | CORNELIA HOFMANN
CORNELIA HOFMANN

Charles Baudelaire
Die Blumen des Bösen.

Les

FLEURS
DU MAL

Sur ta chevelure profonde
Tief in Dein dichtes Haar geschmiegt,
Aux âcres parfums,
Daraus Gerüche quellen,
Mer odorante et vagabonde
Ein Meer, das duftet und sich wiegt
Aux flots bleus et bruns,
Mit braun' und blauen Wellen,

TITEL   SPEECH RECOGNISING LETTERFORMS   1998
TYPEDESIGN   3DELUXE

☐ M

A B C D E F G H I J K L M

N O P Q R S T U V W X Y Z

☐ T

The smallest unit of a word is the letter. The smallest phonetic unit in language is the phoneme. The sound of a vowel or a voiced consonant is extremely individual. 3Deluxe's unusual *Speech Recognising Letterforms* project uses these links as a complex metaphor for making visible audio phenomena – thus discovering associations between acoustics and optics. The frequency and amplitude spectrum of language – in the narrower sense of the word's smallest units – are represented visually by the typeface as letter variations. Thus the vertical axis corresponds with volume (dB) and the various frequencies (MHz) with the horizontal time axis. For example, the letter "A" seems extremely lively, changing, breathing and varying in its heights and depths.

TYPE   BOX   2003
TYPEDESIGN   TETSUYA TSUKADA / HIDECHIKA
DISTRIBUTOR DAINIPPON TYPE ORGANIZATION

☐ 20

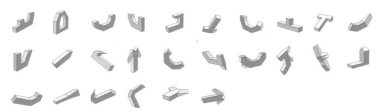

☐ 20

☐ 72

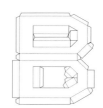

☐ 72

[SOUNDSAMPLE 1 WAVEFORM HAL

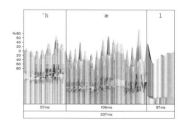

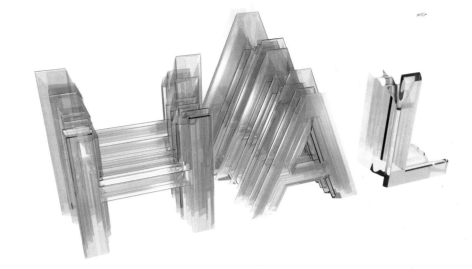

[SOUNDSAMPLE 2 WAVEFORM HAL

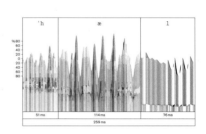

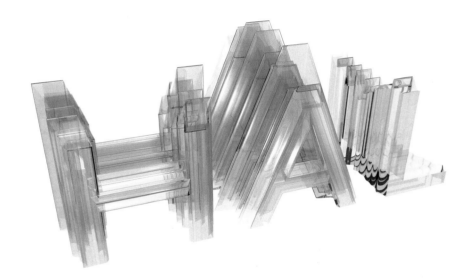

[SOUNDSAMPLE 3 WAVEFORM HAL

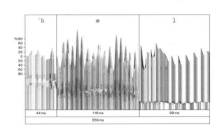

TYPE   OUTSIDE FILL
TYPEDESIGN   RALPH STEINBRÜCHEL
DISTRIBUTOR   WWW.SYNCHRON.CH

1998

[16

ABCDEFGHIJKLMNOPQRSTUVWXYZ
abcdefghijklmnopqrstuvwxyz
0123456789

[8 / 9.5

Lorem ipsum dolor sit amet consectetuer adipiscing elit sed diam nonummy nibh euismod tincidunt ut laoreet dolore magna aliquam erat volutpat Ut wisi enim ad minim veniam quis nostrud exerci tation ullamcorper suscipit lobortis nisl ut aliquip ex ea commodo consequat Duis autem vel eum iriure dolor in hendrerit in vulputate velit esse molestie consequat vel illum dolore eu feugiat nulla facilisis at vero et accumsan et iusto odio dignissim qui blandit praesent luptatum zzril delenit augue duis dolore te feugait nulla facilisi Lorem ipsum dolor sit amet consectetuer adipiscing elit sed diam nonummy nibh euismod tincidunt ut laoreet dolore magna aliquam erat volutpat Ut wisi enim ad minim veniam quis nostrud exerci tation ullamcorper suscipit lobortis nisl ut aliquip ex ea commodo

---

[INSIDE FLOORS   [INSIDE WIRE   [INSIDE FILL

[P

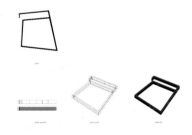

[OUTSIDE ROTATE   [OUTSIDE WIRE   [OUTSIDE FILL

[T

Ralph Steinbrüchel's typographic work was part of a final college assignment. The Swiss designer based this typeface on Daniel Libeskind's design for the extension to London's Victoria and Albert Museum. He developed his four basic faces, *Inside*, *Outside*, *Space* and *Plan*, metaphorically from the internal and external structure of the building. Other faces were described, with the designer focusing mainly on the architectural structures of space and depth.

TYPE	BUDOSI-45	2002
TYPEDESIGN	BONBON / VALERIA BONIN, DIEGO BONTOGNALI	
DISTRIBUTOR	BONBON	

⌐ 16

ABCDEFGHIJKLMNOPQRSTUVWXYZ
abcdefghijklmnopqrstuvwxyz
0123456789-(.,:?+!≠)* «$?%» [/]&@?⇐

⌐ 8 / 9.5

Lorem ipsum dolor sit amet, consectetuer adipiscing elit, sed diam nonummy nibh euismod tincidunt ut laoreet dolore magna aliquam erat volutpat. Ut wisi enim ad minim veniam, quis nostrud exerci tation ullamcorper suscipit lobortis nisl ut aliquip ex ea commodo consequat. Duis autem vel eum iriure dolor in hendrerit in vulputate velit esse molestie consequat, vel illum dolore eu feugiat nulla facilisis at vero et accumsan et iusto odio dignissim qui blandit praesent luptatum zzril delenit augue duis dolore te feugait nulla facilisi. Lorem ipsum dolor sit amet, consectetuer adipiscing elit, sed diam nonummy nibh euismod tincidunt ut laoreet dolore magna aliquam erat volutpat. Ut wisi enim ad minim veniam, quis nostrud exerci

⌐ 12

Budosi45 - Roman
Budosi60 - Italic
Budosi45 - Bold

⌐ 90

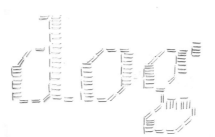
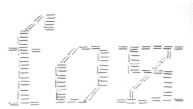

⌐ T

"Every tool leaves its own, specific traces." This is where designers Valeria Bonin and Diego Bontagnali started. Legibility and tradition are not of primary importance, the key is playing "... with the general ideas of the alphabet..." The designer duo distinguish between three phases in the design process; "the tool, the technique, the rule". They produced typefaces including *Budosi*, an entirely legible face, stimulated by the paperclip. The designers' model was the modern font *Bodoni*. The immediate impression *Budosi* makes on the viewer suggests expanding the above-mentioned "tool" concept intellectually to cover material in general.

(The prize-winning book "Typografieren – Atlas" contains a stimulating summary of important typographic work by Valeria Bonin and Diego Bontagnali. Here, among other things, the common test sentence – *The quick brown fox jumps over the lazy dog* – is used playfully and stretched as a metaphor to include reconnoitring foxes in a territory that has been marked out typographically and cartographically.)

TYPE   BUDOSI-BLACK   2002
TYPEDESIGN BONBON / VALERIA BONIN, DIEGO BONTOGNALI
DISTRIBUTOR BONBON

[20

ABCDEFGHIJKLMNOPQRSTUVWXYZ
abcdefghijklmnopqrstuvwxyz
0123456789-(.,:?+!#)* «??%» [/]&@?‹=›

[8 / 9.5

Lorem ipsum dolor sit amet, consectetuer adipiscing elit, sed diam nonummy nibh euismod tincidunt ut laoreet dolore magna aliquam erat volutpat. Ut wisi enim ad minim veniam, quis nostrud exerci tation ullamcorper suscipit lobortis nisl ut aliquip ex ea commodo consequat. Duis autem vel eum iriure dolor in hendrerit in vulputate velit esse molestie consequat, vel illum dolore eu feugiat nulla facilisis at vero et accumsan et iusto odio dignissim qui blandit praesent luptatum zzril delenit augue duis dolore te feugait nulla facilisi. Lorem ipsum dolor sit amet, consectetuer adipiscing elit, sed diam nonummy nibh euismod tincidunt ut laoreet dolore magna aliquam erat

[60

quick

TYPE   VALORA   2001
TYPEDESIGN OPALE / PASCAL DUEZ

[20

ABCDEFGHIJKLMNOPQRSTUVWXYZ
0123456789

[8 / 9.5

LOREM IPSUM DOLOR SIT AMET CONSECTETUER ADIPISCING ELIT SED DIAM NONUMMY NIBH EUISMOD TINCIDUNT UT LAOREET DOLORE MAGNA ALIQUAM ERAT VOLUTPAT UT WISI ENIM AD MINIM VENIAM QUIS NOSTRUD EXERCI TATION ULLAMCORPER

[P

[8 / 9.5

B4S

[8 / 9.5

DESIGN   BONBON / VALERIA BONIN, DIEGO BONTOGNALI
TYPE   BUDOSI—BLACK
PHOTO   OLIVER LANG, ZÜRICH / LENZBURG 2003

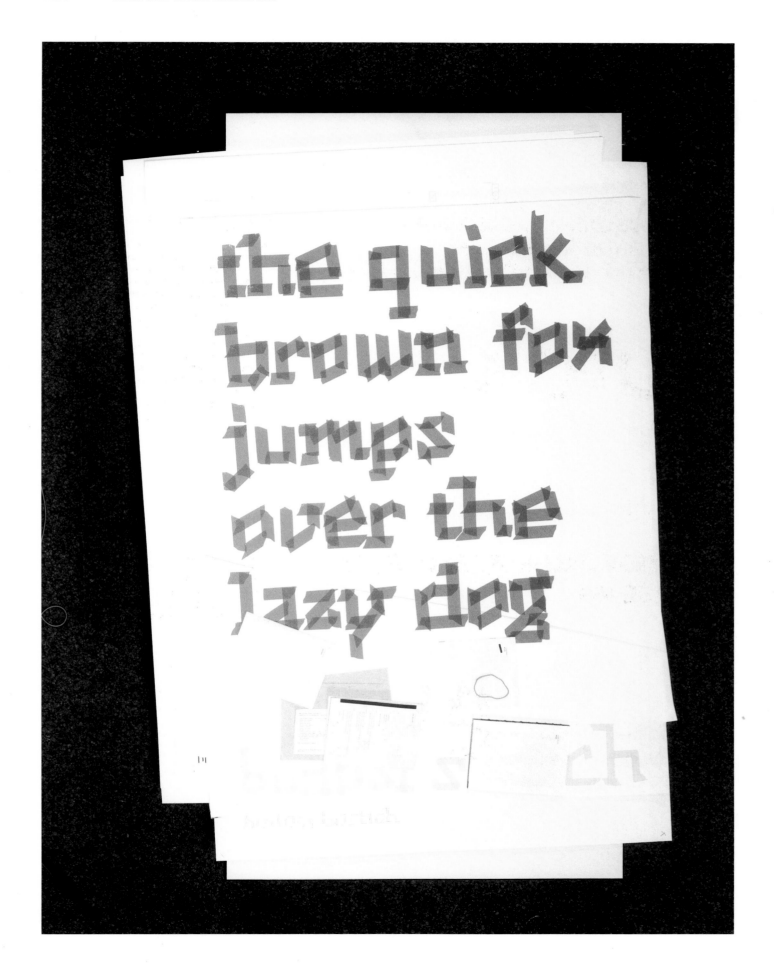

TYPE ADHESIVE
TYPEDESIGN FULGURO

2003

C 16

ABCDEFGHIJKLMNOPQRSTUVWXYZ
abcdefghijklmnopqrstuvwxyz
0123456789-(.,:?+!#)*«$£%»[/]&@ß‹=›

C 12

Adhesive-Normal
Adhesive-Medium
Adhesive-Medium Italic
Adhesive-Bold
Adhesive-Bold Italic
Adhesive-Black

C 120

C NORMAL   C MEDIUM   C BOLD   C BLACK

C 8 / 9.5

Lorem ipsum dolor sit amet, consectetuer adipiscing elit, sed diam nonummy nibh euismod tincidunt ut laoreet dolore magna aliquam erat volutpat. Ut wisi enim ad minim veniam, quis nostrud exerci tation ullamcorper suscipit lobortis nisl ut aliquip ex ea commodo consequat. Duis autem vel eum iriure dolor in hendrerit in vulputate velit esse molestie consequat, vel illum dolore eu feugiat nulla facilisis at vero et accumsan et iusto odio dignissim qui blandit praesent luptatum zzril delenit augue duis dolore te feugait nulla facilisi. Lorem ipsum dolor sit amet, consectetuer adipiscing elit, sed diam nonummy nibh euismod tincidunt ut laoreet dolore magna aliquam erat volutpat. Ut wisi enim ad minim veniam, quis nostrud exerci tation ullamcorper suscipit lobortis nisl ut aliquip ex ea commodo

C T

The *Adhesive* typeface was created – as a result of a witty idea – while a poster was being designed for the "Les Urbaines" art festival. It is based on words and letters "written" with adhesive tape. These letters were fixed to a wall, then photographed and digitised, thus creating a complete character set by using a computer. The designers quite deliberately left the material qualities of the adhesive tape – like torn ends or irregularities – as part of the face. The complete fonts then formed the basis of all of the festival's design media – and for the printing of the adhesive tape intended for stickers.

TYPE NB FORM
TYPEDESIGN NEUBAU / STEFAN GANDL
DISTRIBUTOR WWW.NEUBAULADEN.COM

2003

C 20

ABCDEFGHIJKLMNOPQRSTUVWXYZ
abcdefghijklmnopqrstuvwxyz
0123456789-(.,:?+!#)*«$£%»[/]&@ß‹=›

C 8 / 9.5

TYPE   PATRIOT KIT SADAM
TYPEDESIGN BORIS KAHL
DISTRIBUTOR WWW.VOLCANO-TYPE.DE, WWW.MAGMA-KA.DE

2002

[16

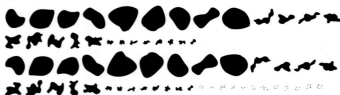

[8 / 9.5

TYPE   PATRIOT KIT SLOBODAN
TYPEDESIGN BORIS KAHL
DISTRIBUTOR WWW.VOLCANO-TYPE.DE, WWW.MAGMA-KA.DE

2002

[18

[8 / 9.5

TYPE   PATRIOT KIT GEORGE
TYPEDESIGN BORIS KAHL
DISTRIBUTOR WWW.VOLCANO-TYPE.DE, WWW.MAGMA-KA.DE

2002

[20

[8 / 9.5

[T

Con Magma's *Patriot Kit* type-set is a gentle satire on current military and political events and design trends. Con Magma asks; "What is all this supposed to be; camouflage-look baby rompers, camouflage girlie shirts?" So the *George* font was created in a subjective and artistic examination of the current US administration. The border of Europe and America supply the basis for ornamental-looking letter shapes. Colour variations and superimpositions suggest new "world pictures" and "camouflage patterns".

TYPE   RUSSISCH BROT   1997
TYPEDESIGN HELMUT NESS UND MARKUS REMSCHEID
DISTRIBUTOR WWW.LINOTYPE.COM

⌐ 16 RUSSISCH BROT ⌐AT ⌐TWO

ABCDEFGHIJKLMNOPQRSTUVWXYZ
abcdefghijklmnopqrstuvwxyz
0123456789–(.,?!/\)'«€£%»¡/¡&@ß←=→

⌐ 8 / 9.5 USSISCH BROT ⌐AT ⌐MIX

Lorem ipsum dolor sit amet, consectetuer adipiscing elit, sed diam nonummy nibh euismod tincidunt ut laoreet dolore magna aliquam erat volutpat. Ut wisi enim ad minim veniam, quis nostrud exerci tation ullamcorper suscipit lobortis nisl ut aliquip ex ea commodo consequat. Duis autem vel eum iriure dolor in hendrerit in vulputate velit esse molestie consequat, vel illum dolore eu

⌐ REGULAR   ⌐ ONE   ⌐ TWO   ⌐ THREE

TYPE   JAVAL DREYFUSS-TWOPOINTS   2001
TYPEDESIGN FRANÇOIS RAPPO (CHARLES DREYFUSS, EMILE JAVAL, 1905)
DISTRIBUTOR PRIVATE FONT

⌐ 18

abcdefghijklmn·pqrstuvwxyz
–.,

⌐ 8 / 9.5

lorem ipsum dolor sit amet, consectetuer adipiscing elit, sed diam nonummy nibh euismod tincidunt ut laoreet dolore magna aliquam erat volutpat. ut wisi enim ad minim veniam, quis nostrud exerci tation ullamcorper suscipit lobortis nisl ut aliquip ex ea commodo consequat. duis autem vel

⌐ 100

⌐ T

The French type designer François Rappo's *Javal-Dreyfuss* typeface is an attempt to capture the historic experimental designs by Emile Javal (c. 1900). Charles Dreyfuss had already done some drawing work on these designs in the 1920s, with his eye on the pictorial effect of a complete word, and Rappo emphasises this.

abcghv

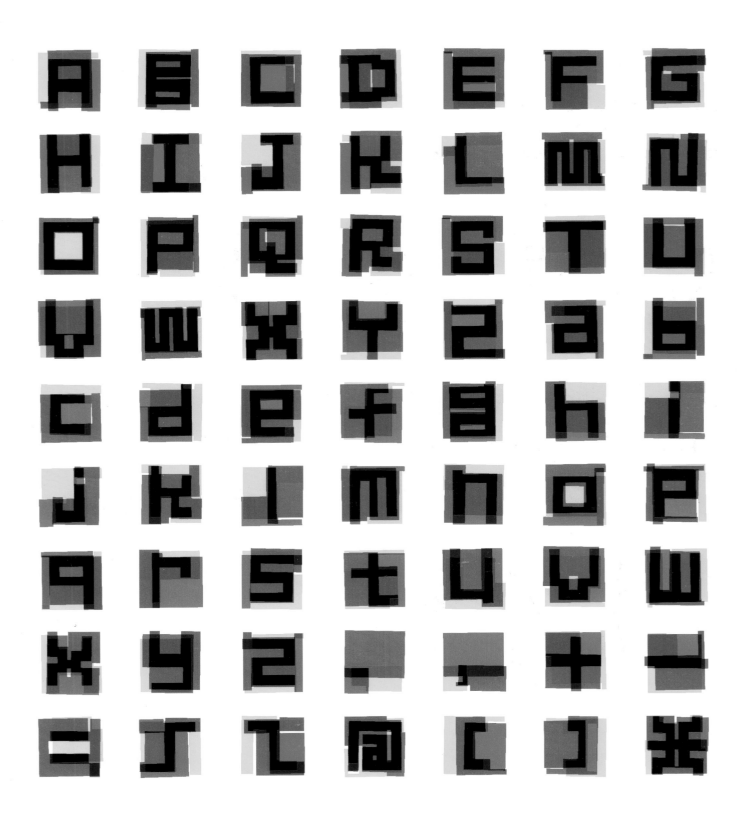

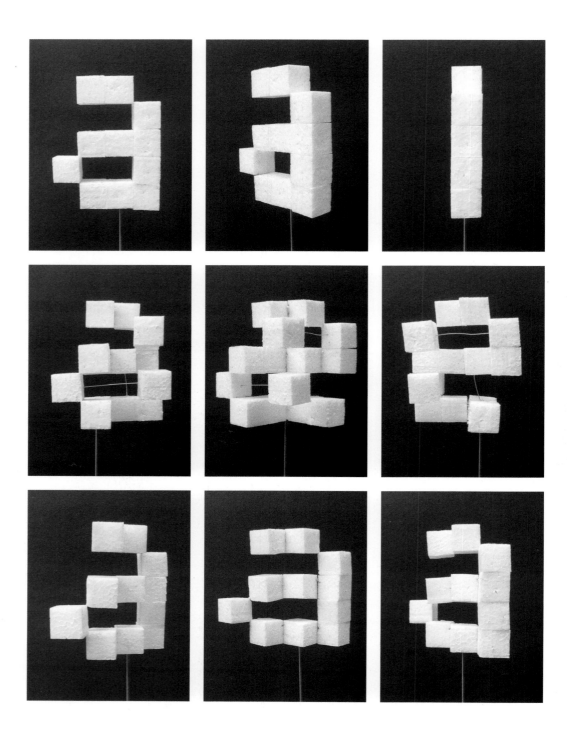

–
⌐ T

Theres Jörger's impressive work called "Typografie und
Raum" emerged as part of a piece of research. She
extends our ways of looking at pieces of typography,
as sensually perceptible objects in space, by adding
the third dimension. Typography and language acquire
depth that can be grasped in a way that is spatially
complex and ambiguous. Theres Jörger divides her
wide-ranging analysis into five variants: evolution,
alphabet, construction module, boxes and mutants;
here are some examples.

–
⌐ ↗

She creates different statements by turning the master
models through 90 degrees around the vertical axis.
So turning master model two through 90 degrees leads
from "a" via "æ" to "e", while a 90-degree turn of master
model three simply changes the proportions of the
letter "a". In this way it is possible to combine two
pieces of letter-information in one three-dimensional
object, or to retain a single piece of information by a
90-degree turn.

DESIGN   THERES JÖRGER
TITEL   TYPOGRAFIE UND RAUM
YEAR   2001

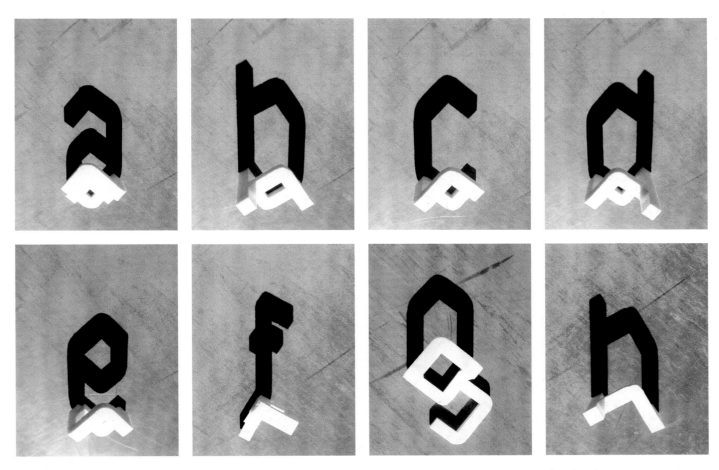

↗

Light and shade become the central theme.
If a letter is at a certain angle to the sun it produces a
two-dimensional copy as a shadow.

↘

The illustration shows variants on the letter "e" from a
number of angles. This is a continuation of the original
model.

When the observer reads from differing eye levels
or distances the perception of forms and proportions
changes.

Words and their subject-matter are reduced to mere
object status by dissecting and nesting the letters. The
message, which was originally clearly defined, mutates
into an ambiguous cipher.

TYPE INBETWEEN   2004
TYPEDESIGN JUTOJO
DISTRIBUTOR WWW.DIE-GESTALTEN.DE

⌐ 22   ⌐ 72

abcdefghijklmnopqrstuvwxyz
abcdefghijklmnopqrstuvwxyz
0123456789-~...?+y/@

jazz

TYPE LIN   1998
TYPEDESIGN HANSJACOB FEHR

⌐ 18   ⌐ 72

ABCDEFGHIJKLMNOPQRSTUVWXYZ
0123456789-.,:!

auto

TYPE DEADTYPE   1999
TYPEDESIGN HANSJAKOB FEHR
DISTRIBUTOR WWW.LINETO.COM

⌐ 16   ⌐ T

The designer cannibalised an old typewriter he had taken to pieces for his signs. He then digitalised this arbitrarily created "type matter" and used it as the basis for a type alphabet.

⌐ 80

 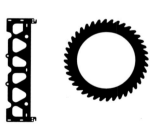 

DESIGN   JUTOJO
TYPE   INBETWEEN
PHOTO   JUTOJO

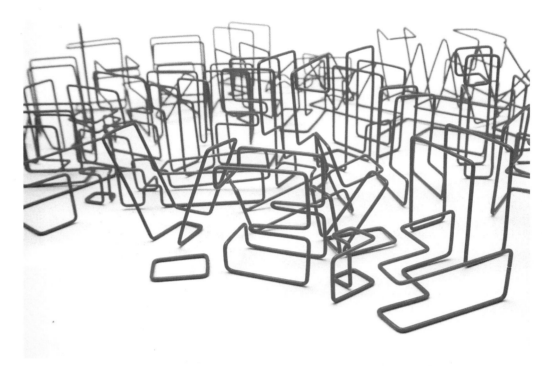

DESIGN   HANSJACOB FEHR
TYPE   LIN

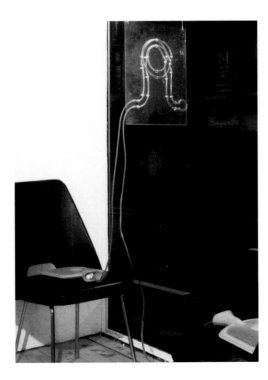

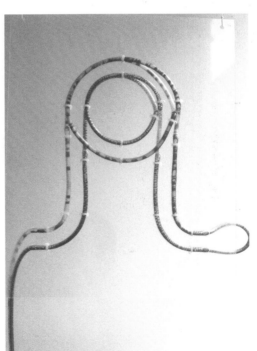

TITLE   TRUE TYPE
AUTHOR   NORM, MANUEL KREBS / DIMITRI BRUNI
CHARACTERS 11.677

Copy: Our typography teacher wore a black shirt with a narrow, white leather tie, and white leather shoes. He spoke Basel German. This man – the same person who had initiated us into the secrets of the logo –, made us copy manuscripts with a quill pen: the *Capitalis Monumentalis*, the *Carolingian Minuscule*, the *Unzial* and the *Rustika*. The work was demanding and dull. We couldn't see the point of the exercise, the leather tie was bigger than the subject, we got out of it as much as we could. Most people handed in work done by students in the previous year, as the exercise was always the same. There was a proper trade in successful manuscripts by older students, so you do well on the course if you had a good relationship with the higher classes. Then in the second term we were supposed to draw individual characters in *Helvetica* with paintbrush and plaka. Here too we did nothing but scoff at the exercise. We wanted to draw big, expressive images, not to perfect the circle connection in a letter "n". And so our first year went by; we didn't know what we were doing. A bit later there was a crucial incident in the copying room. Student A, who was in the diploma class, had left a few sheets lying around in a heap with the copies that had gone wrong. On it was a bold typeface that A had designed. The fact that you can draw a whole typeface made us nervous. A became our idol. We admired A, and imitated his work from then on. One evening we made a key discovery, the school was practically empty, we had a good look round the diploma year's classroom. We found a book called "The Graphic Language of Neville Brody" on A's desk. A had taken over Brody's work – Brody was a graphic designer we didn't know about –, in every detail. We realised we had copied a copy of a copy. The typeface that A was supposed to have drawn was Neville Brody's *FF Typeface Six*, a crude version of *Futura* with pointed ends on N, M, V and W. When we were on the preliminary course there was only one computer in our school, but stocks were built up over three years and soon there were ten Quadras in the computer room. Our teacher refused to use computers, which made them all the more interesting. We approached them tentatively, you could fit a whole term's work on to a single floppy disk. When we were in the diploma year the first copies of Fontographer appeared. No one knew how this program worked. We made our first typeface without knowing about Metrics Window, without any preview of the typeface, we just drew the outlines and generated the typeface. This is like a woodcutter felling a tree with the chainsaw switched off. Our results were extremely primitive.

Old whores: Our typefaces are still primitive, and the longer we work with typefaces the more difficult it seems to take up a clear position. Sometimes we wish we had the certainty of our teacher with the white leather tie. He worked with two typefaces throughout his lifetime, *Univers* and *Akzidenz Grotesk*. We reject you out of hand, you are old whores. But everyone used them; they were once perfect and now they have been sucked dry.

We reached a point at which we decided it was impossible to work with typefaces that already existed. All the typefaces over a hundred years old were absolutely out of the question, they came from another era, and were not appropriate to our times. We were convinced that a design that was appropriate to its times should not use forms that are a hundred or two hundred years old. This eliminated a large number of typefaces; so that left the twentieth century ones. And there were not many of those we respected or were interested in.

That's how things were for us, and we drew up the following guidelines:
1. We only work with typefaces we have drawn ourselves. (Only a typeface you have drawn yourself can be appropriate to the use you are going to make of it, that is the only way to achieve unity of typeface and design.)
2. Every commission needs its own typeface, no typeface may be used twice. (This is like wearing a fragrance, it is highly irritating if one piece of work suddenly smells like another.)

By now we had discovered Metrics Window. In our first euphoria, which lasted for some time, we generated a number of pixel and matrix typefaces. We made quick, crude fonts. That was all right as long as we were doing flyers; you were halfway there with the typeface. But we were soon confronted with a dilemma. We were not producing enough new typefaces and at the same time we started having doubts about our own forms. We either had to make better typefaces or broaden our typographical horizon.

Boy bands: There are two kinds of typefaces, those made by typographers and those made by graphic designers, drawn typefaces and constructed typefaces, body-text typefaces and title typefaces. You can make a typeface in a day, indeed in an hour, but you can work on a typeface for a year as well. Typographers concentrate exclusively on the typeface. When their typeface is finished their mission is over and they hands their product over to a user. Typographers are aware of the burden of typeface history, they strive for perfection, their aim is to achieve harmony and legibility. Graphic designers are typeface barbarians, they usually make typefaces for themselves. They are interested in application, and go all out for effect; for them form comes before function. The two should not be played off against each other. The fact that the two approaches run in parallel is nothing new, graphic designers have always created their own typefaces for posters. Typefaces that were very short-lived and sometimes used only once. At the same time it can be said with certainty that a typeface like *Biff* definitely makes more impact on a poster that *Syntax*, for example. Perhaps it's best to compare the two approaches with classical and popular music; a typographer's whole family of typefaces would be comparable with a symphony, while the graphic designer is writing a pop song. Perhaps graphic artists who make typefaces should be compared with singer-songwriters. The fact that an immense number of typefaces are available is a new phenomenon. Shorter-lived typefaces now have something that used to be reserved for classical typefaces. So we have the major labels like Fontshop, for example, that cover the whole bandwidth. Fontshop's enormous range also explains our complete lack of interest in this sales operation, their selection is undiscriminating, they have something of everything, the best and the worst. Then there are the smaller labels, like Optimo or Lineto, for example; associations of young men (there is no saying why most of the people who make typefaces are men) who go for a more focused selection. The typefaces offered are a statement, the small range on offer confirms the quality of their selection and the attitude behind the sales operation.

Grotesque: Designing typefaces is still part of our working process. We usually start with the typeface; that is to say we first prepare the design tool. We're not quite as categorical about it any more; we've been using existing – including classical – typefaces for about two years now. But we're still designing typefaces and developing what we demand of them. There's not as much time now for our own designs, certainly, but this remains part of our approach. First, we have the typeface, then we design. We tend to work longer on a typeface – no more fast faces. And yet we are less interested in the laborious process leading to a complete family of typefaces than in wanting to put an idea or a principle into practice. We will always be typeface-constructors and not typographers, we are not qualified to be the latter. We sell only a very small number of our type-faces. There are three reasons for this:
1. There are typefaces we don't want to sell because they are our personal tools. We don't want to share with anyone, letting them go would be like someone selling his own child.[3]
2. A second reason for not wanting to sell typefaces is that we are dubious about their quality. If we can't use them ourselves we don't want to pollute the whole world with them. Presumably this is what happens to most typeface designers, five font-corpses for one accept-able typeface, attempts left by the wayside that would actually be almost acceptable, but somehow aren't right.[4,5]
3. The third reason is that a lot of staying power is needed to produce an acceptable typeface. Getting a typeface ready to sell involves a lot of work. The typeface must meet the right standards, be well-drawn (constructed), hinting and kerning have to be treated with the appro-priate dedication. Making a typeface decently acceptable is no joke.

We still have a lot of unanswered questions, but we can say for certain that the typeface is the key element in every design. It is the com-ponent that influences the product's character most crucially. Thus the choice of typeface is the most important of all creative decisions. The designer is at the mercy of the typeface – the typeface is the programme.

1   Norm: Was ist ein Logo? Los Logos. Berlin, dgv, 2002.
2   *Biff* v. *Syntax*.
3   *Hammer*, a semimonospaced typeface, there are three widths instead of one, one unit for narrow characters (I ! , . : ;), three units for broad ones (M W) and two units for all the other characters. We have used this typeface a great deal for large and gigantic jobs, and also made a stencil version and a somewhat more elegant one.
4, 5 *Standard* and *Rhodesia, Standard* was a very ambitious project, a con-structed response to *Unica*, which was probably bound to fail. The roman face was almost complete, there was to have been a special (in addition to the planned thin, medium, bold and black) in the form of another face, *Standard-vector*. This face would have worked through line thickness rather than colour, and would have made it possible to repro-duce the typeface in a hairline weight. It would have been a good idea but we didn't implement it strongly enough. We had drawn *Rhodesia* completely, (working with Maxime Bücji and Aurèl Sack). This typeface is based on the road signs in Harare, Zimbabwe. We had planned it for a catalogue, but somehow the typeface had suddenly taken on a life of its own and was not right for the catalogue any more. We never used either of these typefaces.

SimpelKoelnBonn, this typeface was a redesign of *Simple* that we made at Rudi Baur's request for the signage at Cologne-Bonn airport. The monospaced *Simple* was reconstructed as a proportional typeface. We ended up by redrawing all the characters (with the exception of o). Work on *SimpelKoelnBonn* took four to five months.

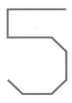

CHAPTER   GRID
AUTHOR   SILJA BILZ
CHARACTERS   878

Using a grid in typography is not new (type area, base line grid). The grid has proved useful in type design when building up an homogeneous alphabet. Grids make it possible to impose order on design information within a consistently uniform matrix, without the structure of the grid being superficially perceptible. And yet this ordering principle – both in typography and in modern architecture and art – is consciously used as an aesthetic stylistic device. Crude grid forms in particular have provided typographical and aesthetic inspiration in a whole variety of ways down to the present day – we remember the abundance of current pixel types. The following chapter gives examples of quite different approaches to using the grid as a formal and artistic principle.

GRID

TYPE HAMMER-BOLD   2001
TYPEDESIGN NORM

⌐ 16

ABCDEFGHIJKLMNOPQRSTUVWXYZ
0123456789
– (.,:?+!) *h%./_&℮<=>

⌐ 8 / 9.5

LOREM IPSUM DOLOR SIT AMET, CONSECTETUER
ADIPISCING ELIT, SED DIAM NONUMMY NIBH
EUISMOD TINCIDUNT UT LAOREET DOLORE MAGNA
ALIQUAM ERAT VOLUTPAT. UT WISI ENIM AD
MINIM VENIAM, QUIS NOSTRUD EXERCI TATION
ULLAMCORPER SUSCIPIT LOBORTIS NISL UT
ALIQUIP EX EA COMMODO CONSEQUAT. DUIS
AUTEM VEL EUM IRIURE DOLOR IN HENDRERIT IN
VULPUTATE VELIT ESSE MOLESTIE CONSEQUAT,
VEL ILLUM DOLORE EU FEUGIAT NULLA FACILISIS
AT VERO ET ACCUMSAN ET IUSTO ODIO DIGNISSIM
QUI BLANDIT PRAESENT LUPTATUM ZZRIL DELENIT

⌐ M

HAMMER
FETT!NM

1 2 3

⌐ 12

HAMMER-BOLD
STATETHIS

TYPE A NEW FONT   2002
TYPEDESIGN OLAF NICOLAI, STEPHAN MÜLLER (PRONTO)
DISTRIBUTOR WWW.LINETO.COM

⌐ 12

⌐ T

The graphic designer Olaf Nicolai makes two main points in his *A New Font* project. Firstly, he identifies the medial character of Utopian concepts, and secondly he defines artistic production "as a process involving shared work and contradictions", whose result "is open to various appropriations!" According to his view of type, every element within a letter can accommodate three colours – and the colour scheme itself can be selected by the user. The designer programmed a complete set of type matter on the basis of this idea.

⌐ 96

- -

TYPE   MACARONI
TYPEDESIGN   FLAG
DISTRIBUTOR   WWW.FLAG.CC

2001

◰ 16 MACARONI ALT FILLED-MEDIUM

ABCDEFGHIJKLMNOPQRSTUVWXYZ

abcdefghijklmnopqrstuvwxyz

0123456789-(.,:?+!#)*«$£%.»[/]&@ß<=>

◰ 8 / 9.5

Lorem ipsum dolor sit amet, consectetuer
adipiscing elit, sed diam nonummy nibh euismod
tincidunt ut laoreet dolore magna aliquam erat
volutpat. Ut wisi enim ad minim veniam, quis
nostrud exerci tation ullamcorper suscipit lobortis
nisl ut aliquip ex ea commodo consequat. Duis
autem vel eum iriure dolor in hendrerit in

◰ 72 MACARONI-UP, MACARONI-LIGHT, MACARONI-DOWN

◰ 12

MacaroniAlt-Down
MacaroniAlt-Light
MacaroniAlt-Medium
MacaroniAlt-Medium
MacaroniAltFilled-Medium

- -

TYPE   DOOR2DOOR
TYPEDESIGN   MARTIN WOODTLI

2003

◰ 18

ABCDEFGHIJ LMNOPRSTU W Y -
0123   6789.:

◰ T

Swiss graphic designer Martin Woodtli's typeface is
immediately attractive thanks to impressively three-
dimensional effects in the appearance of the type.
Effects of depth and contrast are enhanced by
superimposing various type levels in combination with
colours and textures.

◰ M

- -

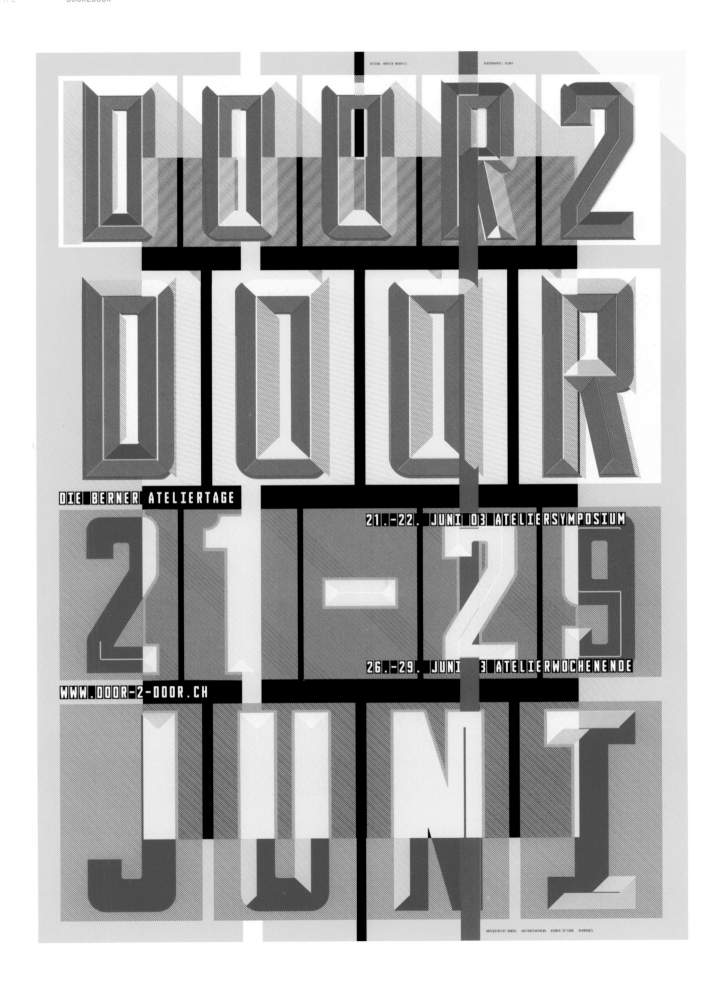

TYPE	FILE SHARING	2003
TYPEDESIGN	RICHARD NIESSEN	
DISTRIBUTOR	FREE DOWNLOADABLE	

⌐ 24

⌐ 8 / 9.5

ABCDEFGHIJKLMNOPQRSTUVWXYZ
abcdefghijklmnopqrstuvwxyz
0123456789g

Lorem ipsum dolor sit amet, consectetuer
adipiscing elit, sed diam nonummy nibh euismod
tincidunt ut laoreet dolore magna aliquam erat
volutpat. Ut wisi enim ad minim veniam, quis
nostrud exerci tation ullamcorper suscipit
lobortis nisl ut aliquip ex ea commodo
consequat. Duis autem vel eum iriure dolor in

TYPE	STYREN	2002
TYPEDESIGN	FULGURO	

⌐ 18

⌐ 8 / 9.5

ABCDEFGHIJKLMNOPQRSTUVWXYZ
abcdefghijklmnopqrstuvwxyz
1234567890

TYPE	ANZARA-VERTICAL	2002
TYPEDESIGN	PIERRE ROESCH	
DISTRIBUTOR	HTTP://WWW.TYPOTEK.COM	

⌐ 18

⌐ 8 / 9.5

ABCDEFGHIJKLMNOPQRSTUVWXYZ
abcdefghijklmnopqrstuvwxyz
0123456789-(,.:?+!#)* «<$£%>» [/]&@□<=>

Lorem ipsum dolor sit amet, consectetuer adipiscing elit, sed
diam nonummy nibh euismod tincidunt ut laoreet dolore magna
aliquam erat volutpat. Ut wisi enim ad minim veniam, quis
nostrud exerci tation ullamcorper suscipit lobortis nisl ut
aliquip ex ea commodo consequat. Duis autem vel eum iriure
dolor in hendrerit in vulputate velit esse molestie consequat,
vel illum dolore eu feugiat nulla facilisis at vero et accumsan et

⌐ 60

anzara

⌐ 60

anzara

⌐ 12

Anzara Normal
Anzara Optique
Anzara Vertical
Anzara Optique

Anzara Double
Anzara Circuit

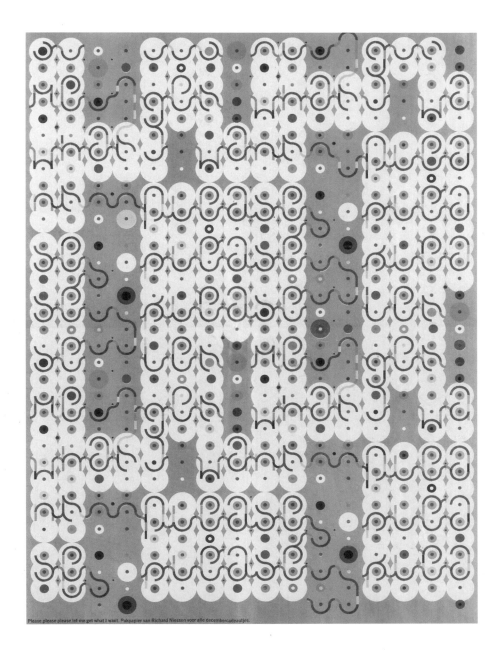

Please please please let me get what I want. Pakpapier van Richard Niessen voor alle decembercadeautjes.

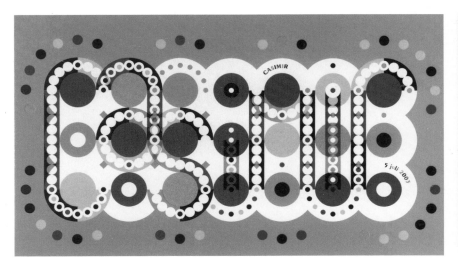

TYPE   MODUL ALFA01   2002
TYPEDESIGN LUKA MANCHINI
CREDIT   PROF. LUCIJAN BRATUS

▭ 16   ▭ 8 / 9.5

ABCDEFGHIJKLMNOPQRSTUVWXYZ   **MODUL ALFA 01**

abcdefghijklmnopqrstuvwxyz   MODUL ALFA 02

0123456789-(.,:?+) [/]<>   MODUL ALFA 03

                                                    MODUL ALFA 04

▭ ALFA1   ▭ ALFA2   ▭ ALFA3   ▭ ALFA4   ▭ 130

TYPE   CROSSWIRE   2002
TYPEDESIGN LUKA MANCHINI
CREDIT   PROF. LUCIJAN BRATUS

CROSSWIRE5   ▭ 72

ABČDEFGHIJKLMNOPQRŠTUVWXŽY

▭ CROSSWIRE4

ABČDEFGHIJKLMNOPQRŠTUVWXŽY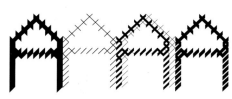

▭ CROSSWIRE3

ABČDEFGHIJKLMNOPQRŠTUVWXŽY

▭ CROSSWIRE2

ABČDEFGHIJKLMNOPQRŠTUVWXŽY   ▭ 72

▭ CROSSWIRE1

ABČDEFGHIJKLMNOPQRŠTUVWXŽY

DESIGN   NON-FORMAT / KJELL EKHORN & JON FORSS
TYPE   CUSTOM MADE / HELVETICA
PHOTO   JAKE WALTERS

DESIGN   LUKA MANCHINI
TYPE   CROSSWIRE

//////// font: Crosswire
//////// leto: 2002   //////// status: neaktiven   //////// stran 1

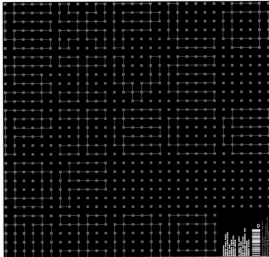

TYPE GAIJIN-SHADOW 2002
TYPEDESIGN BORIS DWORSCHAK
DISTRIBUTOR WWW.STEREOTYPEHAUS.COM

☐ 16 ☐ 8 / 9.5

abcdefghijklmnopqrstuvwxyz
ABCDEFGHIJKLMNOPQRSTUVWXYZ
0123456789-(.,:?+!) «£» (/16⬛◇)

Lorem ipsum dolor sit amet,
consectetuer adipiscing elit, sed
diam nonummy nibh euismod tincidunt
ut laoreet dolore magna aliquam erat
volutpat. Ut wisi enim ad minim
veniam, quis nostrud exerci tation
ullamcorper suscipit lobortis nisl ut

TYPE ONTHESPOT 2000
TYPEDESIGN MARTIN WOODTLI

☐ 18 ☐ T

Martin Woodtli's work is characterised by a preference
for isometric presentation and three-dimensional
structures using contemporary typeface characteristics.
Computer and keyboard are his most important tools.
He deliberately breaks up two-dimensional planes,
modifies them playfully and exploits them typographically.

☐ 18 ☐ 8 / 9.5 ☐ 8 / 9.5

☐ 18 ☐ 8 / 9.5

DESIGN   BORIS DWORSCHAK
TYPE   GAIJIN-SHADOW
PHOTO   MATTHIAS HALLER

DESIGN   MARTIN WOODTLI
TYPE   ONTHESPOT

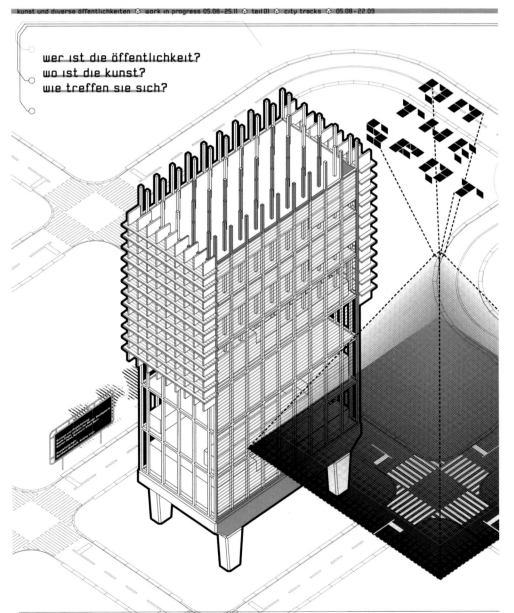

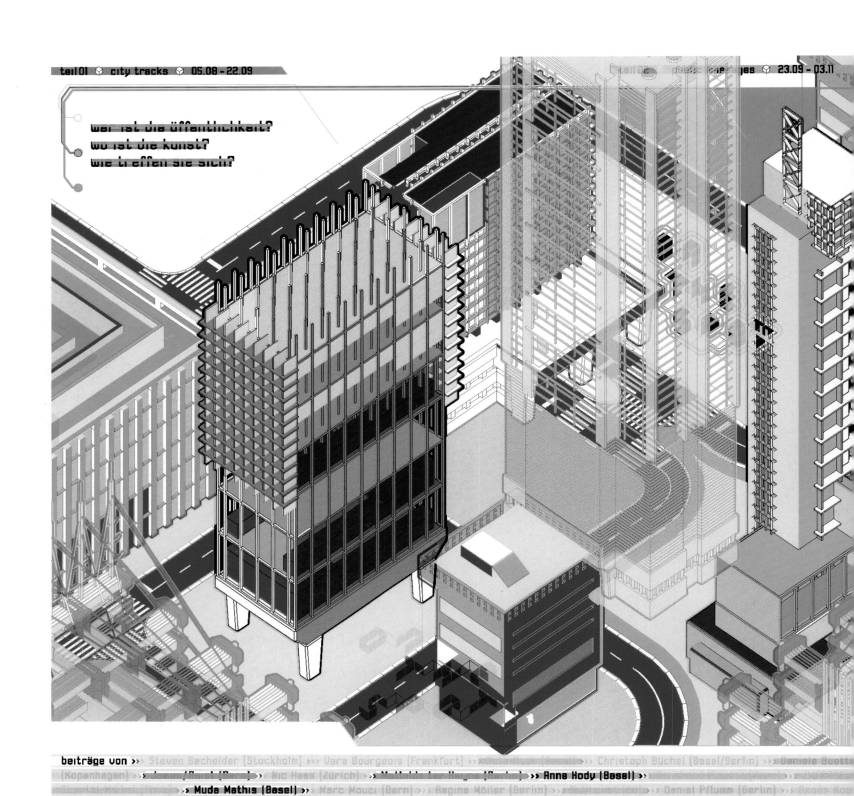

teil 01 ⬡ city tracks ⬡ 05.08 - 22.09

teil 02 ⬡ public passages ⬡ 23.09 - 03.11

wer ist die öffentlichkeit?
wo ist die kunst?
wie treffen sie sich?

beiträge von ›› Steven Bachelder [Stockholm] ››› Vera Bourgeois [Frankfurt] ››› .... ››› Christoph Büchel [Basel/Berlin] ››› Daniela Buett [Kopenhagen] ››› Jonny/Roist [Bern] ›› Nic Hess [Zürich] ››› Mathilde ter Heijne [Berlin] ›› Anne Hody [Basel] ›› ›› Muda Mathis [Basel] ›› Marc Mouci [Bern] ›› Regina Möller [Berlin] ››› Daniel Pflumm [Berlin] ››› .... Michael Stauffer [Bern] ››› Stöckerselig [Basel] ›› S.U.S.I. mit Peter Brand, Martin Guldimann u. Andres Loux [Zürich/Bern] ›› Sybille Walpen [Bern] ››

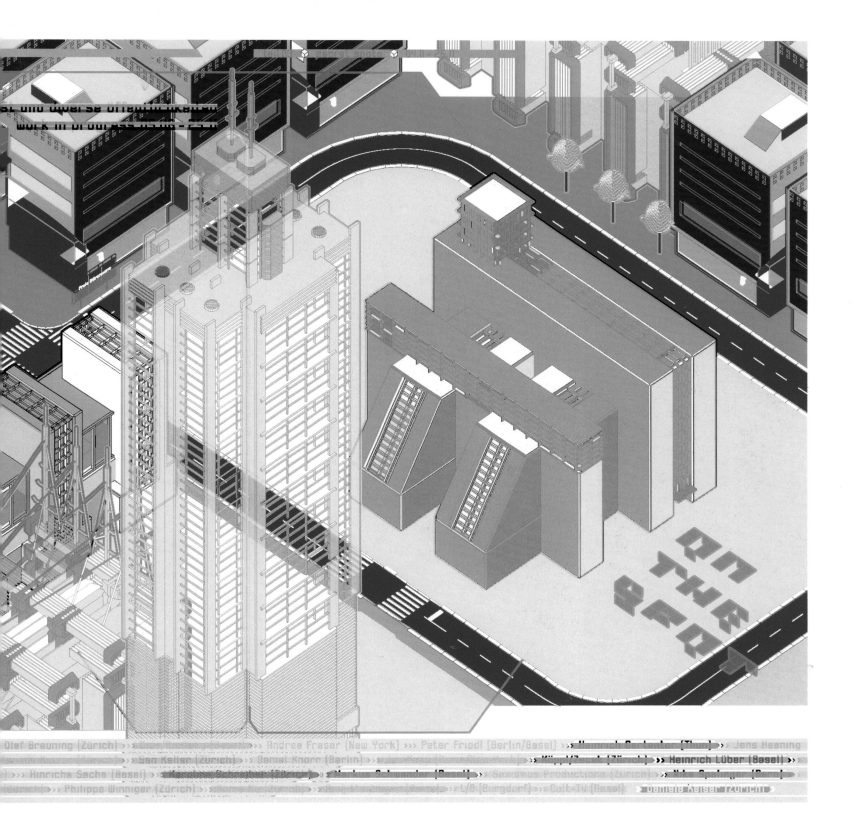

TYPE   CUBE   2003
TYPEDESIGN   TETSUYA TSUKADA / HIDECHIKA
DISTRIBUTOR   DAINIPPON TYPE ORGANIZATION

⊏ 72   ⊏ 72   ⊏ 72

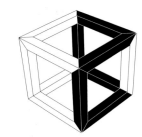 

⊏ 12

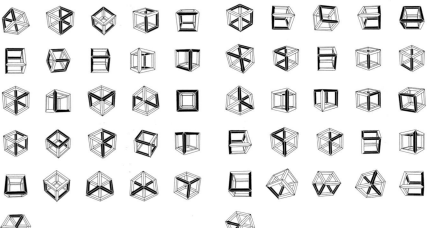

TYPE   BUILDING-AL   2004
TYPEDESIGN   MASAYUKI SATO
DISTRIBUTOR   MANIACKERS DESIGN / WWW.MKS.JP.ORG

⊏ 14   ⊏ 72

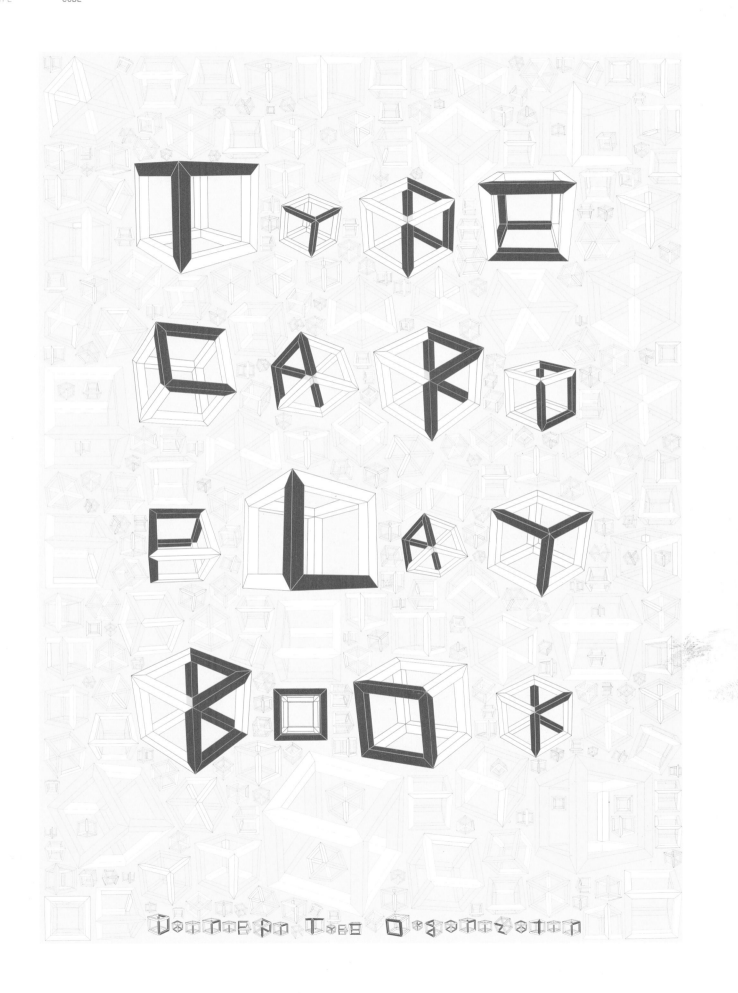

TYPE   VERSAILLES
TYPEDESIGN   IZET SHESHIVARI

2002

⌐ M

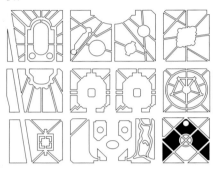

⌐ T

Some people discover certain structures and forms in apparently unstructured, chaotic patterns; the artist Izet saw letters in the gardens of the Palace of Versailles, and used the garden ground plan as the matrix for his typeface. To do this he examined the letter structures he had discovered and photographed the letters' succinctly expressive corners or crossovers.

⌐ M

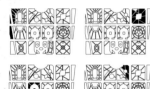   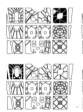 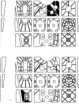   

⌐ M

La promenade du Roi

⌐ 20 LE BOSQUET ROYAL

ABCDEFGHIJKLMNOPQRSTUVWXYZ
abcdefghijklmnopqrstuvwxyz
0123456789-.,?!&()

⌐ 9

VERSAILLES   BOSQUET LA GIRANDOLE
VERSAILLES   LES DEUX FONTAINES
VERSAILLES .. LE THEATRE D· EAU
VERSAILLES .. L· OBELISQUE
VERSAILLES   NOUVEAU LABYRINTHE
VERSAILLES   ROYALE

TYPE   SMR REGULÄR
TYPEDESIGN   BODARA, BÜRO FÜR GEBRAUCHSGRAFIK / TOBIAS PEIER

2001

⌐ 18

ABCDEFGHIJKLMNOPQRSTUVWXYZ
1234567890⌐,⌐;-_/!?@[]<>

⌐ P

⌐ 120

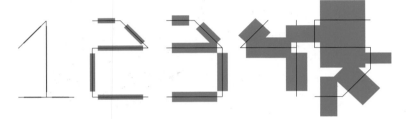

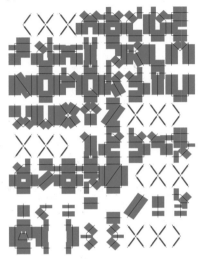

TYPE   LU-REGULAR
TYPEDESIGN   HAPPYPETS

2003

⌐ 14

ABCDEFGHIJKLMNOPQRSTUVWXYZ
abcdefghijklmnopqrstuvwxyz
0123456789-.,?!⌐<>←→⌐■◆■■□■⊞
■⊟⊞⊟⊟■■■■■■■■■■■■■■■■■■■■

⌐ 8 / 9.5

Lorem ipsum dolor sit amet, consectetuer
adipiscing elit, sed diam nonummy nibh euismod
tincidunt ut laoreet dolore magna aliquam erat
volutpat. Ut wisi enim ad minim veniam quis nostrud
exerci tation ullamcorper suscipit lobortis nisl
ut aliquip ex ea commodo consequat. Duis autem vel
eum iriure dolor in hendrerit in vulputate velit

TYPE   KEYBOARD
TYPEDESIGN   BONBON / VALERIA BONIN, DIEGO BONTOGNALI
DISTRIBUTOR   BONBON

2001

⌐ 20

AbcdEFGHIJKLM
NOPQRSTVVWXYZ

⌐ 8 / 9.5

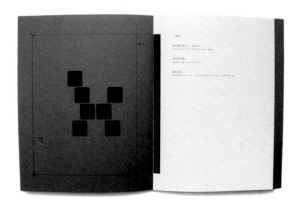

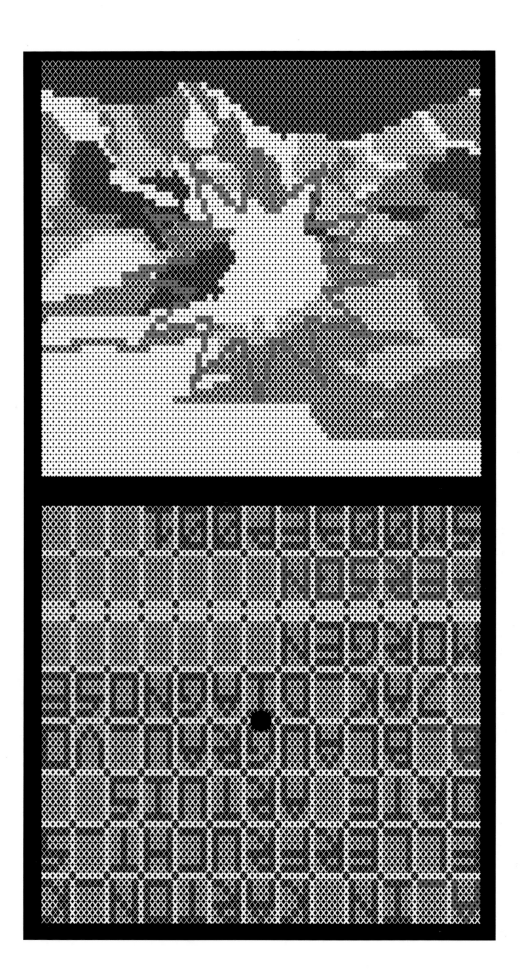

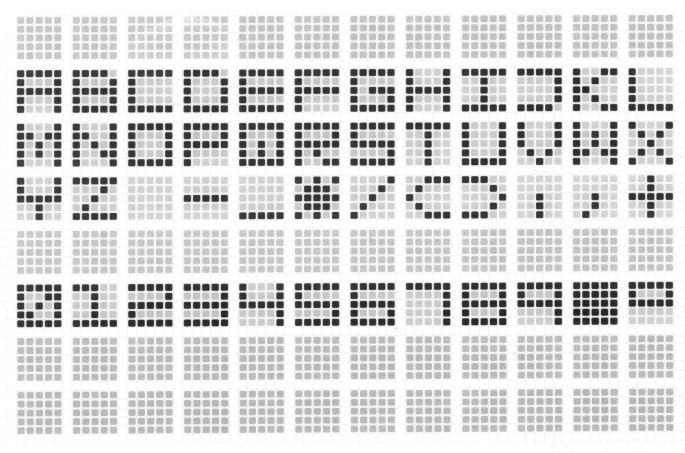

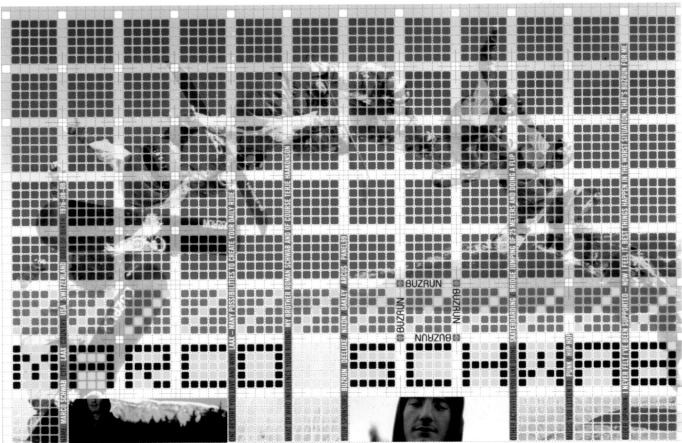

TYPE TWIN CITIES 2003
TYPEDESIGN KONTOUR DESIGN / SIBYLLE HAGMANN

⌐ 24

ABCDEFGHIJKLMNOPQRSTUVWXYZ
abcdefghijklmnopqrstuvwxyz
0123456789-[.,:;?+!#]

⌐ T

How can certain qualities of a major city be conveyed through a typeface? Various typographers were faced with this question as the brief for an international competition to design a new typeface for the twin cities of Minneapolis and St. Paul. Designer Sybille Hagmann's solution is based on the idea of building perspective and depth – as typical elements of an urban landscape – into the typeface design. She developed a mathematical and geometric concept corresponding with the well-known space co-ordinates x, y, z. She also added bowls to individual letters to work against the visual austerity of the typeface. The result is that the typeface concept has various features in its appearance. Sibylle Hagmann explains that she tried to use the individual appearance of the type to convey characteristic architectural elements of the two cities – e.g. the Victorian style in St. Paul or "the massive presence of the skyscrapers", in downtown Minneapolis.

⌐ 12

Cities

⌐ 12

TwinCities Regular
TwinCities Script
TwinCities Super
▶▶▶llI◀◀◀ᛁᚷᛁlᛁ¹⁰● TwinCities Element

⌐ 12

▶▶▶llI◀◀◀

TYPE FRAC 2003
TYPEDESIGN RE-P / NIK THOENEN

⌐ 15

ABCDEFGHIJKLMNOPQRSTUVWXYZ
↖↖↘↘↗↗↙↙←↓←◇→^→‹ →← >⹀
0123456789-[.,:+!] [/]&@

⌐ 6 / 8

LOREM IPSUM DOLOR SIT AMET, CONSECTETUER ADIPISCING ELIT, SED DIAM NONUMMY NIBH EUISMOD TINCIDUNT UT LAOREET DOLORE MAGNA ALIQUAM ERAT VOLUTPAT. UT WISI ENIM AD MINIM VENIAM, QUIS NOSTRUD EXERCI TATION ULLAMCORPER SUSCIPIT LOBORTIS NISL UT ALIQUIP EX EA COMMODO CONSEQUAT. DUIS

⌐ 48

⌐ 12

FRAC-THIN
FRAC-LIGHT
FRAC-REGULAR
FRAC-MEDIUM
FRAC-BOLD
FRAC-EXTRA

DESIGN   RE-P / NIK THOENEN
TYPE   FRAC
PHOTO   LISA RASTL / PASCAL PETIGNAT

LE NOUVEAU LIEU
DU FONDS RÉGIONAL D'ART CONTEMPORAIN
DE LORRAINE

49 NORD 6 EST   FONDS RÉGIONAL D'ART CONTEMPORAIN DE LORRAINE
1 RUE DES TRINITAIRES   F-57000 METZ   TÉL 0033 3 8774 2002 / FAX 0033 3 8774 2056

H

TITLE   TYPE IN MOTION
AUTHOR   PREVIEW / TANJA DIEZMANN
CHARACTERS   12.114

In the field of animated typography, the technical developments of the last few years have stimulated designers to exploit visual potential to the full, thus producing a large number of new aesthetics and innovative ideas. But this process also produced countless design variants aimed mainly at visual effects. The result was world-wide experimentation and a close juxtaposition of good and bad examples, followed by the lethargy that can be observed at present. If we turn the television on today – never mind what country we are in – it seems as though there have never been any fundamental typographical principles, to say nothing of giving thought to whether typography on the screen should perhaps have to meet different requirements, thus offering different creative possibilities from those that apply to print. As a rule, text is pushed across the screen in lines, it is twisted, zoomed or morphed, provided with special effects to attract more attention, but not so that it can communicate more of the subject matter.

This process is typical of newly developing media and technologies; something similar happened after the invention of lithography. This new process made it possible to reproduce very thin lines, so typefaces of varying line weights were developed and used to grade text hierarchically for poster and advertising design. As well as this, typefaces were created that worked mainly with effects like shadows, line textures or ornaments, to attract the reader's attention. The consequence was a jumble of types of varying quality, and a bewildering diversity of typographic solutions. And not least, this development led to a desire and demand for correctly set typography for functional purposes. This was formulated over the years by William Morris, Peter Behrens and Jan Tschichold and the rest is history. In terms of moving images or digital typography in general we are at precisely the same point as that muddle. So we have to address the question of what digital typography's functional purpose can be today.

Perhaps seeing, or viewing, and reading are contradictions. Even though it has been impossible to imagine moving pictures without text ever since the invention of the cinema; whether in title sequences, or in the text panels that conveyed plot and dialogue in the days of silent films and later served to convey accompanying facts, something we still see on television. Reading demands focused attention, other moving objects in the background are disturbing, while the eye wanders to and fro over the screen when viewing a moving image, following the dynamic objects. In moving picture design, typography and background are fundamentally at odds. This is why, when conveying informative texts on television, the actual image has to be calmed with scrolls, panels and masks so that necessary attention can be paid to the text. But it is also necessary to fuse text and image visually, to create unity of text and image and of seeing and reading, as in commercials and film titles. Here the animation of the typography is matched with the moving camera or objects in the moving material. This is done by combining dynamics and form in design terms; by using out-of-focus

movements, for example. The contrasting pair, text and image, are inextricably entwined. Animated typography has either to be visually separated or integrated as appropriate, either independently but parallel with the image, or on and in the image and synchronised with it. It is difficult to handle viewing and reading at the same time; this can be seen most clearly from films with sub-titles, even though the text is not animated. So in the field of moving-image design and in set text, typography serves different purposes. But the first concern must always be to convey a message through text, which is intended to be absorbed rationally or emotionally according to purpose and intention. In news bulletins typography is used mainly to convey information, rationally and usually as key points. Text is inserted unpretentiously, on panels above or below the image. But it is an integral part of the design for rolling news stations, offering the latest news and stock exchange prices continuously, at the same time as the events that have just been reported. Of course this type should be easily and quickly read, and reduced to essential differentiation characteristics. Not all that difficult to do, you might think. But the reality is different. There's often not just one ticker-text, but two, moving at different speeds, complemented by another information panel where two lines of text are swapped over word by word from top to bottom. Each text has a different point size, sometimes it is set in upper-case and accompanied by different characters, coloured and often of various sizes. So this highly off-putting typographical design, which is also not easy to decipher, does not even follow the rules of classical typography, which uses the lowest possible number of different typefaces and point sizes, and derives the necessity for the use of various types, type styles and type sizes from the hierarchy of subject matter. It is often argued that the texts are designed purely functionally, but this does not hold true because even when upper-case characters are used these take 12% more time to read than mixed setting, so the text moves across the screen more slowly and less information is conveyed. This means that typographic design works against the actual intention, especially in the case of rolling news programmes, the aim of which is to convey information functionally so that it can be read rapidly while other material is being broadcast. Viewers are forced to concentrate harder or the text or on the image, as the two components are designed counter-productively.

In films, commercials and television magazine programmes, on the other hand, typography is intended to make an emotional effect as well as conveying a message. Here space and time play their part as the two essential design dimensions for motion graphics. Animated typography can use dynamics and dramaturgy to influence the impact of subject matter not just through its visual appearance, but also through its behaviour; but virtuoso use is seldom made of these possibilities. If it does happen, the Internet makes sure that the sequences are available world-wide, thus promoting global imitation. Probably the most influential example in recent years is Kyle Cooper's title design for the film "Se7en", which triggered a wave of motion graphics aimed at using visual typographic design to convey the message, the story and the mood of the subject matter. At the same time, the aesthetic and the idea of handling title design more intensively and effectively has been copied countless times. So there is a need to use dynamics to make the formal design of typography carry more of the essence of the subject matter; and there is a demand for addressing viewers on an emotional plane by making the text do what it says, or express what it means in visual terms.

And so they do exist, these interesting examples of typographical design in moving images, as many works by Saul Bass and Kyle Cooper show. They were something special, and they still are, because making a greater impact with animated typography rather than with the written word has never become an everyday phenomenon, and has only caught on to a limited extent in the medium of television.

Set text means that the reader's eye has to move. Good typography guides the eye, and leads it from word to word. Something similar occurs in animated type, which uses the dimension of time to offer dynamic and hence more aggressive possibilities for presenting text, and thus for supporting the reading process. Like other motion graphics, animated type can attract all the attention and thus take control. Viewers are much more involved that they would be by static media, as there is a direct time link; an animation or an interactive work runs parallel with their perception processes. This is because of the way we perceive moving objects, which always attract more attention than static ones. Moving objects in a context trigger a visual reflex, in other words a shift to the thing that is moving. Thus viewers can be tied into events at a higher emotional level. Motion graphics designers all too rarely make deliberate use of movement perception principles to stimulate, guide or surprise the viewers' eye. Dynamic typography could take over functional tasks to a much greater extent than it does today, e.g. presenting or ordering subject matter. Animated typography's effect can be enhanced by closely linking reading and listening as activities. Tracking couples sound and text, so that the dynamic of the text is controlled by the dynamic of the spoken word. The animation of the text is directed by analysis of the spoken word. The animation seems familiar, as the natural dynamic of the starting object is retained. This means that language and text can be linked in a new way, and offers a new potential for typographic animation.

Something that Jan Tschichold insisted on for printed typography in "Die neue Typographie" in 1928 could be realised in a different way now by using animated texts; "Each part of a text relates to the other through specific, logical emphases and values that are given from the outset. What the typographer has to do is express that relationship unambiguously and visibly: through differences in size and weight, sequence, colour, photographs etc." In the field of moving-image design, this could be implemented not just through purely formal, but also through structural design in relation to time. As well as conveying messages in a purely rational way, typography could also pass on emotional aspects or information, going beyond the use of varied, visually attractive effects. So dynamic typography could convey meaning, but also volume, emphasis, speed or pronunciation. Typography could go beyond its present role, which is mainly storage, or conveying information, and use dynamics synchronised with language to open up another communication dimension. Typography could lend a new significance to its sound visualisation function (in Western countries) by conveying sounds not just through characters, by also through their behaviour. This could generate new, dynamic word-images that could be "read" or grasped in a new way. The structure of type could be rethought if it is being written and read in real time. The role of letters and words could be questioned. Movement towards animated characters or ideograms could make the laborious deciphering of dynamic typography obsolete, and serve the purpose of communicating a great deal in a short time (television) or in a small space (mobile devices). Animated typography and the way it is integrated into the moving image could have a new part to play.

CHAPTER   HAPTICS
AUTHOR   SILJA BILZ
CHARACTERS 1.651

Haptics (Greek = science of touch) in the context of typography de-
scribes directly touching and feeling objects and spatial arrangements
in a three-dimensional world. It also stands in the broadest sense as a
metaphor for "being touched" on the plane of emotional perception –
or of "grasping" at the intellectual level. The psychomotoric characteristics of handwriting can also be included here. Consequently, haptics
is a basic element of all mental understanding. If tactile and visual
perception are linked, the third dimension can be presented optically in
two dimensions. Haptic feeling and touching leads to a visual grasp,
to recognising and acknowledging an image that the brain has already
stored. But tactile engrams can also contribute to raising sensual
perception without the haptic stimulus having to be perceived directly
– this is how haptic illusions are conveyed on the visual plane. Such
information is presented through light and shade, changes of perspective or also through planes of illustration that are varied and transparent.
Qualities of material structures, surfaces, marks left by tools and
gravures can be simulated haptically in the same way. In an age when
the hand is increasingly shifting into the background as a tool, hand
sketches, hand-written material or even letters drawn freehand become
very personal and unique typographical "fingerprints". The visual image
becomes a complex and sensual experience.

HAPTICS

EACH DO
GMA AP
PEARS
WITH TH
E DEMAN
D OF GEN
ERAL VA
LIDITY.

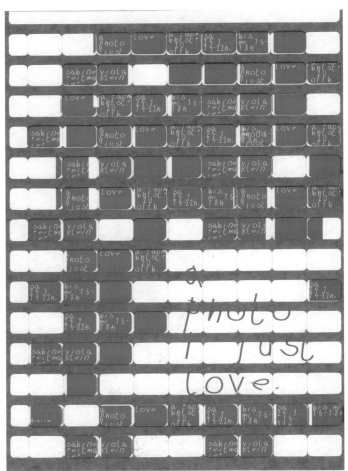

—
DESIGN   FLAG

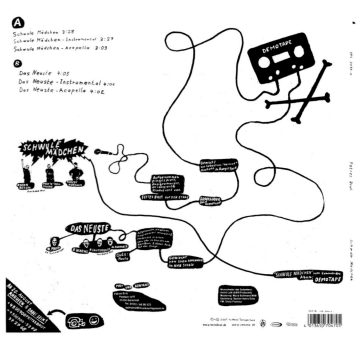

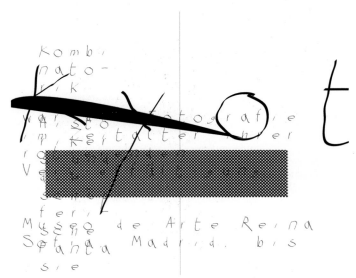

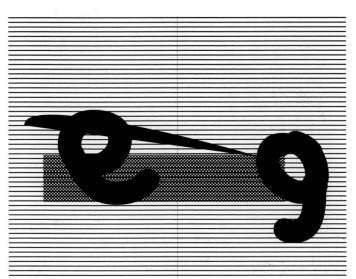

DESIGN MOIRÉ. MARC KAPPELER
ILLUSTRATION CHRIGEL FARNER

—
DESIGN   SEGURA INC.
             CARLOS SEGURA, TNOP, CHRIS MAY, RYAN HOLVERSON
PHOTO   CORBIS

—
DESIGN   SEGURA INC./ CARLOS SEGURA
PHOTO   N/A
—
DESIGN   SEGURA INC./ LAURA HUSMANN, CARLOS SEGURA
PHOTO   N/A

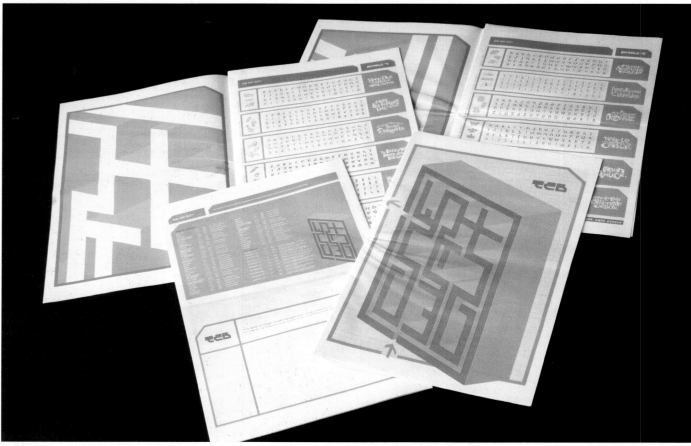

–
DESIGN   SEGURA INC./ CARLOS SEGURA
PHOTO   N/A
–
DESIGN   SEGURA INC./ AKARIT, CARLOS SEGURA
PHOTO   SEGURA INC

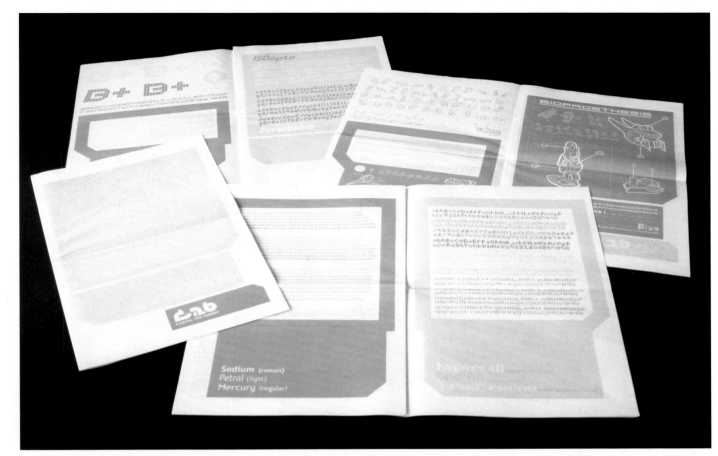

DESIGN   NON-FORMAT / KJELL EKHORN & JON FORSS
TYPE   CUSTOM MADE / MAGDA
PHOTO   SIMON WELLER

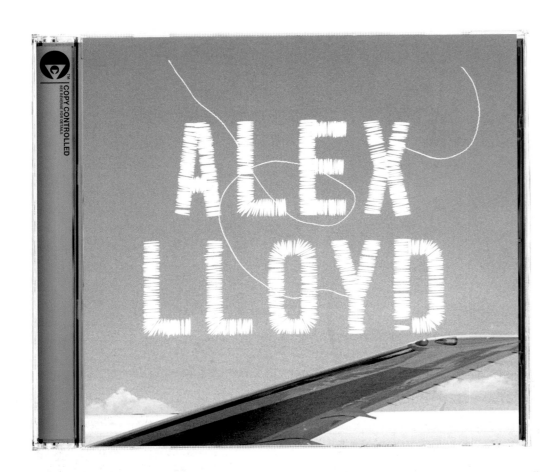

DESIGN   NON-FORMAT / KJELL EKHORN & JON FORSS
TYPE   CUSTOM MADE / MAGDA
PHOTO   SIMON WELLER

BALONY CUP 2003 ENTRÉE GRATUITE
THIS SAMEDILE 24-05
IS DOORS OPEN :
NO KICK OFF : 13H0
AWARD FINAL : 18H30

AVEC :
FC MAGNET
WADTEAM
FG ELECTRONIC
MISSILE   AU STADE CHARLET
             SALLE PIERRE CHARPY
BATOFAR   99, BOULEVARD KELLER
             75013 PARIS — RER CITÉ
AC BALONY
DJ'S DE CHAQUEÉ QUPE :
DIXON (SON KOLLEKTIV, BERLIN)
STEVEN
BLU
P-O, MISTER J. & LES (MISSIVE)
GWEN MAZE (BAT
JOSS DANJEAN
CONTACT : BRICE@BALONYMEDIA.C
ARTWORK : 123BUERO // TIMO G

DESIGN   NON-FORMAT / KJELL EKHORN & JON FORSS
TYPE   CUSTOM MADE / FUTURA
PHOTO   TONY ELLWOOD

Electric Weekend.

Electric Avenue Studios & Ritzy Cinema, Brixton
Saturday 26 June / Sunday 27 June 2004

Electric Weekend celebrates the launch
of b3 media's Electric Avenue Studios
in Brixton with a weekend of free
events at the new venue, plus a film
programme at the nearby Ritzy Cinema.
Supported by the Arts Council England,
b3 media is a non-profit multimedia
arts network fostering innovation and
diversity across the arts.

Over two days, groups and individuals
with shared interventionist
sensibilities will take part in
conversations, workshops,
interventions, tactical media
initiatives, social hacking,
music videos and participatory
artworks. These encounters are geared
towards mapping, connecting and
supporting the diverse media arts
initiatives across London and outside,
focusing on DIY approaches to the
use of public space and technology.

Electric Weekend is a b3 media
production, guest curated by
Lina Dzuverovic-Russell from Electra.
www.electra-productions.com

For further info:
studio@b3media.net
www.b3media.net
020 7278 3131

–
DESIGN   FLAG
PHOTO   FLAG

DESIGN   BÜRO LUDWIG / BIRTE LUDWIG
PHOTO   BIRTE LUDWIG

TYPE   STONE-REGULAR
TYPEDESIGN   THE REMINGTONS
DISTRIBUTOR   CONTACT@THEREMINGTONS.CH
–
DESIGN   UNDERWARE
PHOTO   MAARTEN DE RU @DERU.NU

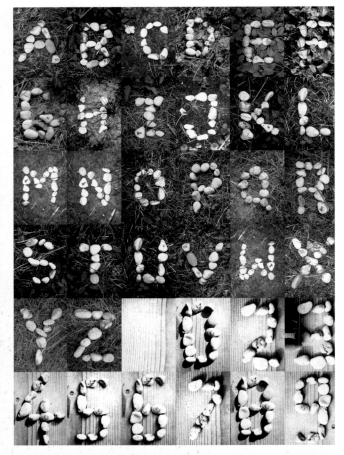

E T

Manuel Reader's "One_Off_Fonts" project looks
ironically at existing Online Fontshops. It is based on a
constantly growing archive of handwriting created by
the designer himself. He emails selected fonts to
interested users free of charge, in Jpeg format or as a
Bitmap version. The poster illustrated refers to this
range.

TITEL   "I COULD HAVE TAKEN AN IMAGE BLOWN IT UP BIG AND PUT BOLD TYPE ON IT.
                BUT I CHOOSE NOT TO." "ONE_OFF_FONTS"

SAGMEISTER INC./ BELA BORSODI
MATTHIAS ERNSTBERGER, MIAO WANG, STEFAN SAGMEISTER
BELA BORSODI

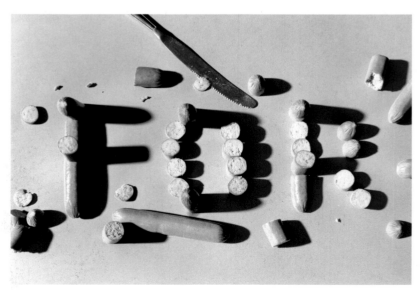

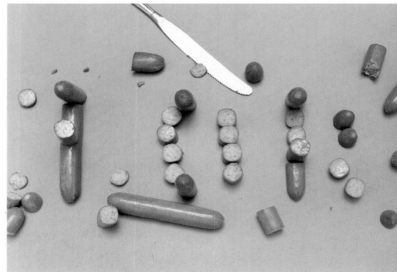

DESIGN   PING PONG
           ANDREA ROCA, FRANZISKA BORN, MARCO WALSER
           IN COOPERATION WITH ISABEL TRUNIGER
TITEL   IN ALPHABETICAL ORDER

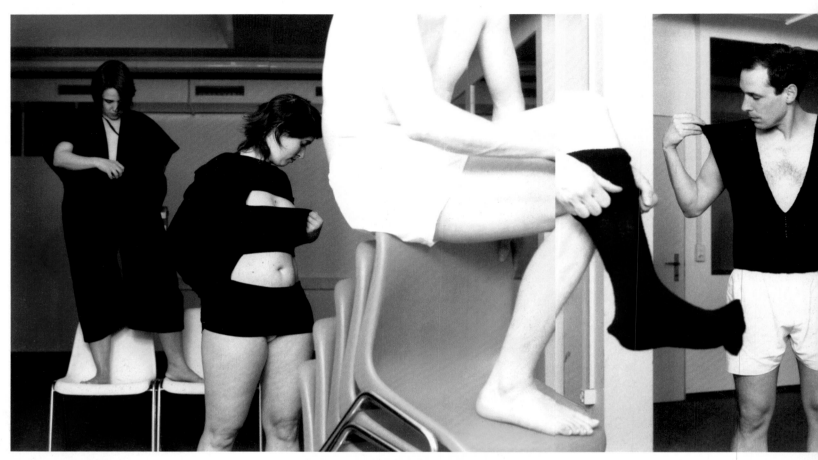

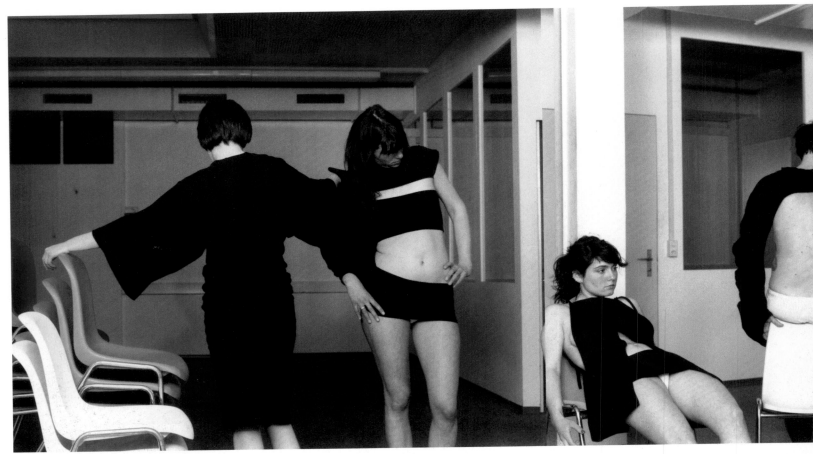

I

–
TITLE   INDEX
CHARACTERS   4.384

0

AGENCY	123Buero
DESIGNER	Timo Gaessner
E-MAIL	hello@123buero.com
WEB	www.123buero.com

AGENCY	1kilo
DESIGNER	Hansjakob Fehr
E-MAIL	ha@1kilo.org
WEB	www.1kilo.org

AGENCY	3deluxe
DESIGNER	Andreas Lauhoff
E-MAIL	a.lauhoff@3deluxe.de
WEB	www.3deluxe.de

A

AGENCY	A´
DESIGNER	Clarissa Tossin
E-MAIL	ola@a-linha.org
E-MAIL	vende_tudo@a-linha.org
WEB	www.a-linha.org

AGENCY	–
DESIGNER	Alexander Wise
E-MAIL	alexander.wise@wanadoo.fr
WEB	–

AGENCY	Atelier télescopique
DESIGNER	–
E-MAIL	atelier-telescopique@wanadoo.fr
WEB	www.ateliertelescopique.com

AGENCY	Attak
DESIGNER	Peter Korsman / Casper Herselman
E-MAIL	attak@attakweb.com
WEB	www.attakweb.com

B

AGENCY	Binnenland
DESIGNER	Mika Mischler
E-MAIL	info@binnenland.ch
WEB	www.binnenland.ch

AGENCY	Bodara / Büro für Gebrauchsgrafik
DESIGNER	Tobias Peier
E-MAIL	bodara@bodara.ch
WEB	www.bodara.ch

AGENCY	BonBon
DESIGNER	Valeria Bonin / Diego Bontognali
E-MAIL	froilein@mails.ch
E-MAIL	diegopop@mails.ch
WEB	www.froilein.ch

AGENCY	–
DESIGNER	Boris Dworschak
E-MAIL	info@borisdworschak.de
WEB	www.borisdworschak.de

AGENCY	Bowling Club
DESIGNER	Bowling Club
E-MAIL	hello@mybowlingclub.com
WEB	www.mybowlingclub.com

AGENCY	Büro Destruct
DESIGNER	Büro Destruct
E-MAIL	bd@bermuda.ch
WEB	www.burodestruct.net
WEB	www.typedifferent.com

AGENCY	Büro Ludwig
DESIGNER	Birte Ludwig
E-MAIL	info@buero-ludwig.com
WEB	www.buero-ludwig.com

C

AGENCY	Cape Arcona Type Foundry
DESIGNER	Stefan Claudius
E-MAIL	general@cape-arcona.com
WEB	www.cape-arcona.com

AGENCY	–
DESIGNER	Cornelia Hofmann
E-MAIL	c_hofmann@t-online.de
WEB	–

D

AGENCY	Dainippon Type Organization
DESIGNER	Tetsuya Tsukada / Hidechika
E-MAIL	dainippon@type.org
WEB	http://dainippon.type.org/

AGENCY	DBXL
DESIGNER	Donald Beekman
E-MAIL	info@dbxl.demon.nl
WEB	www.dbxl.nl

AGENCY	–
DESIGNER	Dirk Wachowiak
E-MAIL	dwac@gmx.net
WEB	–

E

AGENCY	Emigre
DESIGNER	Zuzana Licko
E-MAIL	info@emigre.com
WEB	www.emigre.com

F

AGENCY	FellowDesigners
DESIGNER	Paul Kühlhorn / Eva Liljefors
E-MAIL	paul@fellowdesigners.com
WEB	www.fellowdesigners.com

AGENCY	Floodfonts Freefonts
DESIGNER	Felix Braden
E-MAIL	info@felixbraden.de
WEB	www.floodfonts.com

AGENCY	Flag
DESIGNER	Bastien Aubry / Dimitri Broquard
E-MAIL	info@flag.cc
WEB	www.flag.cc

AGENCY	Fountain
DESIGNER	Felix Braden
E-MAIL	info@felixbraden.de
WEB	-

AGENCY	-
DESIGNER	François Rappo
E-MAIL	-
WEB	-

AGENCY	Fuenfwerken Design AG
DESIGNER	Helmut Ness
E-MAIL	info@fuenfwerken.com
WEB	www.fuenfwerken.com

AGENCY	Fulguro
DESIGNER	Cédric Decroux / Axel Jaccard / Yves Fidalgo
E-MAIL	info@fulguro.ch
WEB	www.fulguro.ch

G

AGENCY	Gul Stue
DESIGNER	Soffi Beier
E-MAIL	soffi@gulstue.com
WEB	www.soffibeier.dk
WEB	www.gulstue.com

H

AGENCY	Handgun
DESIGNER	David Zack Custer
E-MAIL	zack@hand-gun.org
WEB	www.hand-gun.org

AGENCY	Happypets
DESIGNER	Patrick Monnier / Violène Pont / Cédric Henny
E-MAIL	info@happypets.ch
WEB	www.happypets.ch

AGENCY	HardCase Design
DESIGNER	Dmitri Lavrow
E-MAIL	lavrow@hardcase.de
WEB	www.hardcase.de

AGENCY	House Industries
DESIGNER	House Industries
E-MAIL	customerservice@houseind.com
WEB	www.houseindustries.com

I

AGENCY	I O N – Büro für Gestaltung
DESIGNER	Wolfgang Rosenthal
E-MAIL	info@i-o-n.de
WEB	www.i-o-n.de

AGENCY	I.S.K.R.A Werbeatelier
DESIGNER	Vitalij Meier
E-MAIL	v.meier@iskra-berlin.de
WEB	www.iskra-berlin.de

J

AGENCY	-
DESIGNER	Izet Sheshivari
E-MAIL	izet@gmx.net
WEB	-

AGENCY	Jag Och Linus + Lars
DESIGNER	Joel Nordström
E-MAIL	joel@jagochlinus.com
WEB	www.jagochlinus.com

AGENCY	-
DESIGNER	Jean-Jaques Tachdjian
E-MAIL	radiateur@i-c-i.net
WEB	www.i-c-i.net/RADIATEUR

AGENCY	Jutojo
DESIGNER	Jutojo
E-MAIL	info@jutojo.de
WEB	www.jutojo.de

K

AGENCY	KearneyRocholl
DESIGNER	Frank Rocholl
E-MAIL	info@kearneyrocholl.de
WEB	www.kearneyrocholl.de

AGENCY	Kontour Design
DESIGNER	Sibylle Hagmann
E-MAIL	hagmann@kontour.com
WEB	www.kontour.com

I

–
TITLE   INDEX
CHARACTERS   4.384

L

AGENCY	–
DESIGNER	Laurenz Brunner
E-MAIL	laurenz@dreck-records.com
WEB	www.lineto.com

AGENCY	–
DESIGNER	Luka Mancini
E-MAIL	lukamancini@email.si
WEB	–

M

AGENCY	Maniackers Design
DESIGNER	Masayuki Sato
E-MAIL	sato@mks.jp.org
WEB	www.mks.jp.org

AGENCY	–
DESIGNER	Manuel Raeder
E-MAIL	info@manuelraeder.co.uk
WEB	www.manuelraeder.co.uk

AGENCY	–
DESIGNER	Martin Woodtli
E-MAIL	martin@woodt.li
WEB	www.woodt.li

AGENCY	Moiré.
DESIGNER	Marc Kappeler
E-MAIL	marc@moire.ch
WEB	www.moire.ch

AGENCY	Mule Industry®
DESIGNER	Shaharzad Khan
E-MAIL	info@muleindustry.com
WEB	www.muleindustry.com

N

AGENCY	Neasden Control Centre
DESIGNER	–
E-MAIL	info@neasdencontrolcentre.com
WEB	www.neasdencontrolcentre.com

AGENCY	Neubau
DESIGNER	Stefan Gandl
E-MAIL	typen@neubauberlin.com
WEB	www.NeubauBerlin.com
WEB	www.NeubauLaden.com

AGENCY	Non-Format
DESIGNER	Kjell Ekhorn & Jon Forss
E-MAIL	info@non-format.com
WEB	www.non-format.com

AGENCY	Norm
DESIGNER	Dimitri Bruni & Manuel Krebs
E-MAIL	abc@norm.to
WEB	www.norm.to

O

AGENCY	–
DESIGNER	Olaf Nicolai
E-MAIL	nico@snafu.de
WEB	–

AGENCY	Opale
DESIGNER	Pascal Duez
E-MAIL	pascal@opalescent.de
WEB	www.opalescent.de

AGENCY	Optimo
DESIGNER	Gavillet & Rust
E-MAIL	info@optimo.ch
WEB	www.optimo.ch

P

AGENCY	Pfadfinderei
DESIGNER	Critzler
E-MAIL	zelt@pfadfinderei.com
WEB	www.pfadfinderei.com

AGENCY	Pfadfinderei
DESIGNER	Martin Aleith
E-MAIL	zelt@pfadfinderei.com
WEB	www.pfadfinderei.com

AGENCY	–
DESIGNER	Pierre Roesch
E-MAIL	pierreroesch@wanadoo.fr
WEB	http://p.ro.online.fr

AGENCY	Ping_Pong
DESIGNER	Andrea Roca / Franziska Born / Marco Walser
E-MAIL	info@shoppingpong.ch
WEB	www.shoppingpong.ch

AGENCY	Power Graphixx
DESIGNER	Power Graphixx
E-MAIL	support@power-graphixx.com
WEB	www.power-graphixx.com

AGENCY	Products of Play
DESIGNER	Erik Johan Worsøe Eriksen
E-MAIL	erik@playpuppy.com
WEB	www.playpuppy.com

Q

AGENCY	Quinta-feira
DESIGNER	Eduardo Berliner
E-MAIL	eduardo@quinta-feira.org
WEB	www.quinta-feira.org

R

AGENCY	-
DESIGNER	Ralph Steinbrüchel
E-MAIL	steinbruchel@synchron.ch
WEB	www.synchron.ch

AGENCY	Re-p
DESIGNER	Nik Thoenen
E-MAIL	nt@re-p.org
WEB	www.re-p.org

AGENCY	The Remingtons
DESIGNER	Ludovic Balland & Jonas Voegeli
E-MAIL	contact@theremingtons.ch
WEB	www.theremingtons.ch

AGENCY	-
DESIGNER	Rob Meek
E-MAIL	meek@robmeek.com
WEB	www.robmeek.com

S

AGENCY	Sagmeister Inc.
DESIGNER	Stefan Sagmeister
E-MAIL	info@sagmeister.com
WEB	www.sagmeister.com

AGENCY	Segura Inc.
DESIGNER	Carlos Segura
E-MAIL	info@segura-inc.com
WEB	http://segura-inc.com

AGENCY	Selanra Grafikdesign
DESIGNER	Martina Römer / Matthias Nichelmann
E-MAIL	buero@selanra.de
WEB	www.selanra.de

AGENCY	Slanginternational.org
DESIGNER	Nathanaël Hamon
E-MAIL	nat@slanginternational.org
WEB	www.slanginternational.org

T

AGENCY	TM
DESIGNER	Richard Niessen
E-MAIL	richard@tm-online.nl
WEB	www.tm-online.nl

AGENCY	-
DESIGNER	Theres Jörger
E-MAIL	theres.joerger@bluewin.ch
WEB	-

AGENCY	Typotheque
DESIGNER	Peter Bilak
E-MAIL	info@typotheque.com
WEB	www.typotheque.com

U

AGENCY	Underware
DESIGNER	-
E-MAIL	info@underware.nl
WEB	www.underware.nl

V

AGENCY	Vier5
DESIGNER	Vier5
E-MAIL	contact@Vier5.de
WEB	www.Vier5.de

AGENCY	Volcano Type / Magma
DESIGNER	Lars Harmsen / Boris Kahl
E-MAIL	magma@magma-ka.de
WEB	www.volcano-type.de
WEB	www.magma-ka.de

Type One

Edited by Robert Klanten, Mika Mischler, Silja Bilz, Nik Thoenen

Layout and design: Mika Mischler, Nik Thoenen
Display typeface: Frac, type design by Nik Thoenen
Body typeface: T-Star, type design by Mika Mischler
Cover design: Robert Klanten, Mika Mischler, Nik Thoenen

All texts written by Silja Bilz (siljabilz@aol.com) except:

Conversation between Wendelin Hess, Beat Müller,
Wolfgang Weingart by Max Bruinsma
My face or yours? by François Rappo
House Industries interview by Silja Bilz and Robert Klanten
Feature text by Frank Rocholl
Type in motion by pReview / Tanja Diezmann
True type by Norm / Dimitri Bruni, Manuel Krebs

Translated by Michael Robinson
Translation of the House Industries interview by Sonja Commentz
German proofreading by Karla Handwerker
English proofreading by Liz Farrelly

Production management: Janine Milstrey
Editorial support Japan: Junko Hanzawa

Published by Die Gestalten Verlag, Berlin
Printed by Jütte-Messedruck, Leipzig
Made in Germany

Bibliographic information published by Die Deutsche Bibliothek
Die Deutsche Bibliothek lists this publication in the Deutsche
Nationalbibliografie; detailed bibliographic data is available in the
Internet at http://dnb.ddb.de.

ISBN 3-89955-056-0 (English version)
ISBN 3-89955-066-8 (German version)

For your local dgv distributor please check out:
www.die-gestalten.de

Footnotes page 3 – 4

1 Theorie über Wissen und Sprache, "Wissenschaft als Wahrheitssuche";
   Piper Verlag (2004); "Denkanstöße 2004 – Ein Lesebuch aus
   Philosophie, Kultur und Wissenschaft"

2 Karl Bühler: Piper Verlag (2004); "Denkanstöße 2004 – Ein Lesebuch aus
   Philosophie, Kultur und Wissenschaft"

Footnotes page 64

1 Adrian Frutiger, "Eine Typografie" (1995)
2 Jan Tschichold, "Die Bedeutung der Tradition für die Typografie" (1964)

Sources page 3 – 4

Piper Verlag (2004); "Denkanstöße 2004 – Ein Lesebuch aus Philosophie,
Kultur und Wissenschaft"
Adrian Frutiger (1979); "Der Mensch und seine Zeichen"
Linotype AG, "Zur Geschichte der linearen, serifenlosen Schriften"
Friedrich Friedl, Nicolaus Ott, Bernhard Stein (1998);
"Typography – when who how"
Muzika, František (1965); "Die schöne Schrift" Band I und II
Albert Kapr, Walter Schiller (1977); "Gestalt und Funktion der Typografie"
Erhardt Stiebner, Walter Leonard (1977); "Bruckmann's Handbuch
der Schrift"
Hans Jensen (1958); "Die Schrift in Vergangenheit und Gegenwart"
Typografische Mitteilungen, Sonderheft "elementare typografie" (1986)
Peter Karow (1992); "Schrifttechnologie"
Karl Vöhringer (1989); "Druckschriften"